Architecture
Chicago

Contemporary Architecture and Interiors

125th
Anniversary

Volume 12

Special
Chapter History Edition

Award winners featured in this publication will be
exhibited from November 18, 1994 to March 26, 1994
at the Chicago Historical Society.

THE AMERICAN INSTITUTE OF ARCHITECTS
Chicago Chapter

AIA Chicago wishes to express thanks to the following donors without whose generous contributions this Annual would not have been possible.

Co-Sponsors:

Chicagoland Sheet Metal Contractors Association Chicago, Cook and Lake Counties Chapter, SMACNA

Merchandise Mart Properties Inc.

Petersen Aluminum Corporation

USG and Family of Companies

Supporters:

The Chicago Faucet Company

Graham Foundation for Advanced Studies in the Fine Arts

herman miller

Table of Contents

THE AMERICAN INSTITUTE OF ARCHITECTS
Chicago Chapter

AIA

Introduction

A letter from the President

This is a milestone year for AIA Chicago, one of the oldest AIA chapters. One hundred twenty-five years ago in 1869, the Chicago Chapter was chartered by five architects seeking to establish the profession in "the west." W. W. Boyington was elected the first president the same year his famous surviving work, the Chicago Water Tower, was completed. Since then, Chicago architects have made their mark on history, not only in shaping our city, but by influencing architecture throughout the world. Today, Chicago is recognized for its rich architectural heritage and the excellence of those who practice the profession of architecture.

Importantly, the Design Excellence Awards recognize the many individuals associated with a project from its conception to its construction, including the client, contractors, and consultants. Within the architectural firm, a team of professionals collaborate to translate a client's requirements and program into a functioning structure. The practice of architecture today, with complicated building ordinances, new systems technologies and construction methods, and environmental regulations, hardly resembles the nineteenth-century practice familiar to Boyington and his colleagues. But the Chicago architect's chief characteristic for the past one hundred twenty-five years continues to be design leadership. The annual awards pay tribute to design and professional achievements—the best of the best—as selected by leading members of the profession.

This Annual, our twelfth volume, celebrates the excellence of firms practicing today and looks back at the Chapter's history. All entries submitted for review by the juries have been published in the "Submissions" section. In this form, the Annual shows the range of recent work by Chicago architecture and interior architecture firms. The Annual recognizes excellence by students at midwestern schools of architecture and design and also acknowledges outstanding service to the profession. In the future, this Annual will serve as a reference for the wide range of architecture and design produced in the Chicago area during the early 1990s.

The Chapter's anniversary offers an opportunity to reflect upon past accomplishments and future goals. In an effort to examine important historic and contemporary issues related to Chicago's architecture, the "AIA Chicago's 125th Anniversary Lecture Series" brought together historians, critics, and practicing architects in a public forum to talk about buildings, their architects, and their histories. The series has informed the public about the practices and philosophies of twenty-eight award-winning architects and prominent architectural historians. With access to the national AIA's archives in Washington D. C., architect Kathleen Nagle, AIA has researched and written a history of the Chapter from 1869 to the present. Her story emphasizes how frequently the profession's definition and role changed in Chicago, as architects sought ways to regulate building codes, define professional ethics, or contribute to civic improvements.

To mark this anniversary year, I would like to recognize, thank, and encourage all members of the building teams and Chicago's architectural community who strive for excellence.

John H. Nelson, AIA
President, AIA Chicago

Building the Profession:

125 Years of AIA Chicago

Kathleen Nagle, AIA

Beginning in 1869, the Chicago Chapter of the American Institute of Architects has significantly shaped the practice of architecture and the legislative guidelines for the profession and the building trades. Occasionally, historians or architects have recorded the Chapter's history and events. In 1924, Chicago architect Peter B. Wight began a history of the Chicago Chapter of the American Institute of Architects, a story that was updated in a 1929 history edition of the Chapter publication *The Leaflet*. That year marks the end of an important building boom and professional era in the history of Chicago architecture. After the Depression and World War II, the profession would not be the same. The Chicago Chapter AIA's fortunes have varied with the fortunes of its members. On the 125th anniversary of the Chapter, its history provides a look at changing perceptions of the architectural profession from the profession's and the public's point of view.

Photograph of William W. Boyington, by John Carbutt, 1868. Boyington served as AIA Chicago President 1869-1874. (Photograph courtesy of Chicago Historical Society: ICHi-09574)

Presidents	Birthdates	Years in Office
William W. Boyington FAIA	(1818-1898)	1869-74
Peter B. Wight FAIA	(1838-1925)	1874-77
Augustus Bauer FAIA	(1827-1894)	1878-85
Lorenzo D. Cleveland FAIA	(1820-1905)	1885-87
Stephen V. Shipman FAIA	(1825-1905)	1887-88
William Le Baron Jenney FAIA	(1832-1907)	1888-89
John Addison FAIA	(Dates unknown)	1889-90
Stephen V. Shipman FAIA	(1825-1905)	1890-91
Henry W. Hill FAIA	(1852-1924)	1891-92
William Le Baron Jenney	(1832-1907)	1892-93
William W. Clay FAIA	(1849-1926)	1893-94
Samuel A. Treat FAIA	(1839-1910)	1894-95
George Beaumont FAIA	(1854-1922)	1895-96
L. Gustav Hallberg FAIA	(1844-1915)	1896-97
Dankmar Adler FAIA	(1844-1900)	1897-98
Normand S. Patton FAIA	(1852-1915)	1898-99
Samuel A. Treat FAIA	(1839-1910)	1899-1900
William B. Mundie FAIA	(1863-1939)	1900-01
William Le Baron Jenney FAIA	(1832-1907)	1901-02
William Carbys Zimmerman FAIA	(1859-1932)	1902-03
George Beaumont FAIA	(1854-1922)	1903-04

1837–1869: Prehistory

In 1869, the Chicago Chapter of the American Institute of Architects was formed of necessity: to support the profession of architecture, struggling at that time to establish itself as a profession distinct from the building trades. In the mid-nineteenth century the profession of architecture was young. No formal schools of architecture existed in this country until 1869 when MIT was established, soon followed by the University of Illinois in Urbana-Champaign. The emerging profession lacked building regulations, zoning ordinances, and related legislation to shape the profession. Architects competed with builders, especially as the scale of building increased during the nineteenth century.

As early as 1837, when Chicago was only a small collection of frame buildings on Lake Michigan's shore, several men had gathered in New York to form the American Institution of Architects. For the next fifteen years, they met infrequently to discuss the building profession until their charter lapsed. In 1857, twelve East Coast architects met in New York and formally drew up a charter for the American Institute of Architects (AIA). Their goal was to define and advance the profession of architecture.

For its first decade, the AIA was for all purposes a local organization serving architects in New York. In 1867 it reorganized as a national organization with local chapters and held its first convention. After the first year, AIA President Upjohn complained of "too little result" due to the absence of a quorum. John C. Cochrane was the only Chicago member listed in the 1868 convention proceedings. By 1869, the AIA Board of Trustees was courting architects in both Philadelphia and Chicago, trying to persuade them to form local chapters to support their city's architects. Things looked promising, though many resisted high initiation fees ($50) and dues ($20), and many architects believed that architects outside of New York were going to be taxed to benefit New Yorkers. This regional protectionism and competition would continue to divide the profession for many decades.[1]

The history of the Chicago Chapter AIA begins on December 13, 1869 when the AIA Board officially recognized the Chicago Chapter. One month earlier, the

Portrait of Peter B. Wight, by Allen E. Philbrick, oil on canvas, 1913. Wight served as AIA Chicago President 1874-77. (Photograph courtesy of Chicago Historical Society: 1943.54)

Portrait of William Le Baron Jenney, by Walter Ufer, oil on canvas, undated. Jenney served three times as AIA Chicago President: 1888-89, 1892-93, and 1901-02. (Photograph courtesy of Chicago Historical Society: 1943.51)

Presidents	Birthdates	Years in Office
Solon S. Beman FAIA	(1853-1914)	1904-05
Irving K. Pond FAIA	(1857-1939)	1905-06
Arthur F. Woltersdorf FAIA	(1870-1948)	1906-07
Dwight H. Perkins FAIA	(1867-1941)	1907-09
George C. Nimmons FAIA	(1865-1947)	1909-11
Peter B. Wight FAIA	(1838-1925)	1911-12
Elmer C. Jensen FAIA	(1870- 1955)	1912-14
Charles H. Prindeville FAIA	(1868-1947)	1914-16
Frederick W. Perkins FAIA	(1866 -1928)	1916-17
C. Herrick Hammond FAIA	(1882-1969)	1917
N. Max Dunning FAIA	(1873-1945)	1918
Daniel H. Burnham, Jr.	(1886- 1961)	1918
George W. Maher FAIA	(1864-1926)	1918-19
Henry Holsman FAIA	(1866-1961)	1919-21
Albert M. Saxe	(1888- ?)	1921-22
Alfred H. Granger FAIA	(1867-1939)	1922-25

Philadelphia chapter had been chartered, thus making the Chicago Chapter the third oldest chapter in the country. Application was made by its entire membership of five: William W. Boyington, John C. Cochrane, A. H. Piquenard (of Springfield), William H. Drake, and Sanford E. Loring. The architect of the Chicago Water Tower and many other late nineteenth-century buildings, Boyington was elected as the Chapter's first president and named one of three national vice presidents in 1869. The AIA Board issued the Chapter its charter and appropriated fifty dollars to support a library reading room.

The Chicago Chapter accomplished very little before the great conflagration in October of 1871. Before and after the fire, unsatisfactory professional conditions and building standards only encouraged an inferior view of the profession. William Le Baron Jenney, one of the few professionally trained architects in Chicago at the time, complained in 1869 that design was not solely the proprietorship of the trained architect: "Too many buildings are erected without the assistance of an architect...every carpenter considers himself capable of designing a building although he would not undertake any other trade."[2] Although sixty architects were practicing in Chicago, only the Chapter's original five founders were AIA members. At the November 1871 convention in Boston, Chicago delegates complained that their profession was undermined by "little friendly criticism," a lack of general rules and regulations, and no uniformity with AIA rules. As Chapter secretary William Drake continued in his 1871 report, "to overcome these obstacles to the advancement of the best interests of the profession, and of good taste and sound science in building in general, it is considered of the first importance that a better acquaintance with each other should be cultivated."[3] To accomplish this, Chapter members tried to establish a library and reading room. They sorely needed library contributions because most private libraries had been destroyed in the fire.

1870s: Beginnings

Like the history of most of Chicago's buildings, the history of the Chicago Chapter AIA begins after the 1871 fire. The famous disaster was pivotal for architecture in Chicago in obvious ways. One of its first results was to attract talented professionals from the East Coast to meet the sudden demand for all kinds of new buildings. Trained under Upjohn in New York, Peter B. Wight arrived in Chicago three weeks after the fire to view the damage. After reporting his findings to the AIA national convention in November, he moved permanently to Chicago, joining the firm of Carter & Drake. Wight's move prompted John Wellborn Root to relocate from New York to Chicago. Wight had been active in the New York and national AIA, so he and others quickly threw themselves into Chicago Chapter affairs. Throughout the early 1870s, Wight would serve as treasurer, vice president and president for the Chicago Chapter.

Only three months after the fire, the first recorded Chicago Chapter meeting was held on January 11, 1872 at the office of Asher Carter.[4] Understandably, the early meetings were dominated by practical issues affecting fire safety and building construction. The Chapter responded quickly to the crisis of rebuilding a devastated city. A committee was appointed to work with the City Council to write a new fire ordinance. By the end of January, their report was accepted and their suggestions published. In subsequent meetings they discussed foundation requirements and regulation of construction methods in order to strengthen the fire ordinances. The Chicago Chapter's recommendations eventually became the basis of the city's first building ordinance.[5]

Every architect in the city was busy for the first two years after the fire, and the Chapter's membership had more than doubled to twelve. Chicago architects were proud of their accomplishments in raising a new city from the ashes, and the Chapter invited the AIA to hold its annual convention in Chicago in 1873. That year the Chapter moved into its first permanent home on the fourth floor of the Morrison Block. Peter B. Wight later remembered this space as "a very handsome room, plainly furnished and supplied with the conveniences of a club room...It served to show the attendants at the Convention...that the Chapter, though small in numbers, had a home of its own in one of the newly constructed buildings."[6] Apparently the room was little used during the two years the Chapter occupied it, a time when architects complained of unfair professional conditions. In the words of Peter B. Wight:

> "Unscrupulous clients have taken advantage of this state of affairs to drive sharp bargains, whereby they have procured the services of Architects at rates so low that Architects have been forced to resort to a system of collusion with builders and persons furnishing materials, whereby they receive commissions for favors granted, or blood money for neglecting to compel the faithful execution of contracts."[7]

This sentiment expressed the collective frustration of a young profession, before their organization had established standards of ethics.

By the time of the 1873 Convention, Chicago's brief post-fire building boom had collapsed. The national financial crisis of 1873 led to a long economic depression that lasted until 1879 and was especially damaging to the building industry. Still, the Chicago Chapter AIA continued to participate in serious discussion and regulation of the building trades and the practice of architecture. Meetings in 1874, for example, focused on work with the Illinois State General Assembly to perfect the state's lien laws. During the winter of 1875, legislators and architects discussed a proposed new state building law governing cities of 100,000 or more, which meant Chicago. Apparently some were dissatisfied with Chicago's building ordinances and their administration. The Chicago Chapter reported to the 1876 convention that "Owing to municipal corruption it was deemed inexpedient to attempt its passage as a city law through the hands of the Common Council, hence it was placed before the State Legislature, and unfortunately, Chicago politicians accomplished its defeat. There has since passed, through the City Council, a building law with excerpts of the law mentioned."[8]

But the Chapter's initial momentum soon subsided. By 1876, President Wight was scolding members for neglect of Chapter work. Meetings covered subjects of construction and the "honorable" practice of the profession, but were poorly attended; the early organizers of the Chapter were the most active. Worse, the Chapter

had lost members and was finding it hard to recruit new ones, despite dues reductions. Though there were many architects practicing in the city, the Chapter was among the smallest chapters in the country. From 1876 to 1879, meetings were held irregularly . While the economic depression continued, many architects sought new occupations. In 1879, Secretary Samuel Treat reported at the annual convention that the Chicago Chapter membership had dropped to nine.

1880s: Architectural Revival and Professional Controversy

The building boom of the 1880s did not inspire a corresponding revival of professional activities within the Chicago Chapter AIA, even though members were actively interested in affairs concerning the profession. The Chapter's interests seemed directed more toward establishing professional standards. Held infrequently at hotel club rooms, the Chicago Chapter meetings were typically social in nature. Members were not concerned much with regular business and chose not to participate in national AIA affairs. No Chicago representatives attended the conventions of the early 1880s, when all the meetings were held in East Coast cities. In 1883, Secretary Treat wrote that the Chapter had not met in two years.[9] But Chicago architects did force the national AIA to take notice of their increasing influence. As Peter B. Wight remembered, "It was not only a revival of business, but a new spirit had entered into every kind of architecture and its related arts."[10] This "new spirit" in Chicago eventually took the form of a strong regional identity, one marked by a rejection of the national AIA due to a perception that the organization was undemocratic and unfairly biased to favor East Coast architects. Prominent Chicago architects began to voice dissatisfaction with the national AIA.

Architects from cities west of Cleveland sought to create a new organization more responsive to their particular and different concerns. Robert McLean, editor of *Inland Architect*, wrote in May 1884 that "quite an interest is being manifested by the profession in the forming of a Western Association of Architects. A number of prominent architects have made expression, in person or by letter to us, deploring the lack of interest in the West and Northwest in existing organizations, and recommending a distinctively Western association, having kindred aims and being in harmony with present organizations."[11] As a self-selected spokesman for the architects of Midwestern cities, McLean used his editorial influence at *Inland Architect* to endorse the innovative

1921

Following the 1921 national AIA Convention, Howard Van Doren Shaw reported to the Illinois Chapter on the activity of his Chicago colleagues:

"Your delegation filled about six per cent of the chairs in the Convention, but we occupied about fifty per cent of the floor. I say 'we' but figuratively I only held the coats of the gladiators while they went to it. I fear I am a hopeless failure as a delegate. I never changed a by-law in my life. In fact, I did not know anybody ever read constitutions, canons, and by-laws; I thought of them as one does of foundations which one cannot see but hopes are there.

The Canons themselves seem to be for the encouragement of honesty among the architects. If a dissatisfied owner wants to get rid of an architect, or an unprincipled confrere tries to get a job away from you, Canons of Ethics are not likely to help you. You will need a sawed-off shotgun. You cannot legislate a gentleman...I would like to have the Canons graved on old lichen-covered marble. They would be very brief, about like this: 'Be a gentleman if you can, but for God's sake be an architect.' ...

There are notable architects at these conventions, (there would be more if you would emphasize architecture and corral this 'business'), men whose work will go down in history. Why not let them talk of their art and leave the business end to the Board of Directors?....the inspiration of meeting fellow architects and seeing their work would mean real education. The allotted span of life of seventy years is not very long if the first twenty-five are spent in getting ready and the last fifteen in playing golf. It leaves only about thirty years in which to help make this a better looking world than we found it. Let us not spend that remainder in changing by-laws."

Journal of the American Institute of Architects 9 no. 6 (June 1921)

architectural ideals defined by the Western architects. By August 1884, McLean announced a call for architects from the South and West to meet in Chicago in November. By September, over two hundred architects had responded to the call for a new organization more responsive to the needs and goals of architects practicing in western states. To help with the association's first convention, Chicago architect Henry Lord Gay, who was organizing an Institute for Building Arts at the time, offered to pay the new association's expenses, organize a drawing exhibit, and provide a suitable assembly room. On November 12, 1884, when McLean called the first meeting of the Western Association of Architects to order at 15 Washington Street, Daniel H. Burnham was elected temporary chair. The 230 initial members included "most of the distinguished architects in America west of the Allegheny Mountains."[12] The Western Association of Architects continued to function in competition with the AIA for the next five years and was by far the more vital and cohesive architectural organization in the western cities.

In January 1885 the Illinois State Association of Architects was formed as a chapter of the Western Association of Architects, and this group replaced the function of the Chicago Chapter AIA. The group met monthly for symposia and informal discussions on philosophical and practical issues affecting architects. The Chicago Chapter AIA remained in the background after the early 1880s, holding only occasional social and annual meetings. Its membership fluctuated greatly. According to Chapter Secretary William Otis,

> *"Nearly all the members of the Chapter are also connected with the Western Association or the Illinois Association of Architects, both of which bodies are so active in all subjects interesting the profession that our members prefer to make the meetings of the Chapter of the Institute such as to promote friendly feelings between the members rather than for the transaction of much business."[13]*

Relations between the two local organizations were cordial, because most Chicago Chapter AIA members were Western Association members as well. Nonetheless, architects were not well served by two competing organizations whose perceptions of the architectural profession differed significantly.

By 1888, officers of the two groups approached the task of consolidating the two national organizations. Dankmar Adler, Burnham, and others spoke in favor of consolidation to unify different factions of the profession. The Western architects wanted a more democratic organization, one without levels of membership. They wanted an organization with government by members rather than by a board, and they favored a more influential role in shaping goals and by-laws. Chicagoan Stephen Shipman believed that joining the two groups would boost the national AIA with new ideas and energy. This was a widely held opinion, at least among the Western men.

In 1889, the Chicago Chapter AIA and the Western Association of Architects were consolidated in Cincinnati at a joint convention of the two groups, the "consolidation convention." After much discussion of charters, procedure and technicalities, all 375 Western Association members were inducted as Fellows of the AIA. Newly elected national officers for 1890 included John Root as Secretary, Samuel A. Treat as Treasurer, and Dankmar Adler and William W. Clay as members of the Board of Directors. National issues at the time included government architecture, competitions, legal aspects of practice, materials testing and architectural education. In January 1890, the Chicago Chapter AIA and the Illinois State Association of

Members of the Illinois Chapter of the AIA, Chicago Architectural Club, and Chicago Architects's Business Association on an inspection trip to Universal Portland Cement Company in Buffington, Indiana on June 20, 1911. (Photograph courtesy of the Chicago Historical Society: ICHi-24566)

Architects merged into one body, calling itself the Illinois Chapter of the AIA. As a result of Chicago architects' efforts to shape their profession, the national AIA was forced to take notice of their increasing local influence on the profession of architecture.

1890s: Back to Business

After the resolution of organizational differences, Chicago Chapter meetings were held more frequently. The immediate topic was Henry Lord Gay's offer to the Chapter of his Institute for Building Arts at 63-65 Washington Street. From 1890 until 1898 the Chapter again had a permanent home, and it assumed management of the exhibition space and met in the Institute's club room. At this time, the Chapter missed an important opportunity to help with planning for the 1893 World's Columbian Exposition. Despite an eloquent plea by Dankmar Adler, the Chapter's Exhibition Committee failed to carry through with ambitious plans. The Chapter participated primarily as the host to the many architects who came to Chicago for the fair and the AIA annual conventions of 1892 and 1893. Burnham's organizational accomplishment at the the fair earned him great respect among his colleagues, who elected him national AIA president in 1894.

The building boom of the 1880s ended abruptly with the money panic of 1893, during the Exposition. Harsh business realities re-focused the Chapter's interest on bolstering the practice of architecture. Beginning in the 1890s and continuing into the 1920s, chapter members participated in the City Council's discussions about building heights. According to Peter B. Wight in 1924,

"The Chapter always took a conservative view of the questions, on aesthetic grounds opposing the erection of skyscrapers, but recognizing that there were economic questions on which its opinions would not be respected; therefore reserving them. In these discussions the Chapter took the ground that people had the constitutional right to erect buildings as high as they wished to, always provided public safety against fire, collapse and insanitary conditions were provided for, those being debatable questions."[14]

The most important effort for the long-range benefit of the profession was the Chapter's work to pass the Illinois State Licensing Law, the first legislation in the country to regulate the practice of architecture. As early as 1891, Adler had prepared a tentative draft for legislation, but the real effort began in 1895.[15] The Independent Order of the United Bricklayers and Stone Masons of Chicago approached the Illinois Chapter regarding drafting a bill after an accident which they believed was due to an architect's incompetence. A committee headed by William W. Clay was appointed to pursue the issue and its efforts were supported by the building associations. The national AIA forwarded a copy of a licensing bill which had passed the New York Legislature in 1889 but had then been vetoed by the governor. Clay and Peter B. Wight were appointed to draft a bill. Along with Dankmar Adler and Harry B. Wheelock, they continued their efforts until the Illinois Licensing Law was passed in 1897, making it unlawful in the state of Illinois to practice architecture or to advertise oneself as an architect without a license.[16] The legislation also established a Board of Examiners of Architects. Three of the first five board members were Illinois Chapter members and authors of the law: Peter B. Wight, Dankmar Adler, and William Carbys Zimmerman. From its inception, the legislation emphasized safety and was supported by the various building organizations, as it is today. It was not until 1955 that every state had enacted similar architectural licensing laws.

Despite the economic downturn, 1895 and 1896 saw the Chapter active in practical issues such as building heights, the Masons' code, building ordinance violations and enforcement and lien laws. After the annual meeting in September 1896, chapter members initiated plans that would change the Chapter's emphasis. At a separate meeting, architects H. B. Wheelock, Treat, Normand S. Patton, L. Gustav Hallberg, and others suggested that they create a new organization, called the Chicago Architects Business Association, "to fill the long felt desire of the Architects to provide a logical and proper manner for conducting the business side of the profession, inasmuch as the Illinois Chapter declined or neglected to interest itself except on the aesthetic side of architecture."[17] The first recorded meeting of the Association was conducted January 12, 1897 at the club room of the Institute of Building Arts. Most of the original members were also Illinois Chapter members, and they quickly supported the Chapter's work on the licensing bill. The Association was renamed the Illinois Society of Architects in 1914 in order to encourage greater influence throughout the state. For the next several decades, it worked closely with the Illinois Chapter on issues affecting the practice of the profession.

The Monroe Street Bridge as seen in 1994. Photo by Kathleen Nagle, AIA. (Photograph courtesy of the author)

1930

At the 1930 national AIA convention, an observer at the "Symposium on Contemporary Architecture" descibed the heated discussion:

"Promptly at two-thirty the firing broke out again. The battlefield was crowded with morbidly curious spectators, even some members of the fair sex occupying points of vantage in tree tops and balconies. The Referee, who had been dodging all over the place during the morning, now appeared again...and introduced Mr. Earl Reed, Jr., one of the younger gunmen of Chicago. Mr. Reed lived up to the reputation of his village and pretty soon respectable citizens were dodging behind posts, as respectable citizens will, and innocent bystanders were wondering how Louis Sullivan and Dan Burnham got mixed up with Al Capone's boys. Mr. Reed had a lot of 'savoire faire,' and as he twirled his gun, showed how Modernism had been invented in Chicago a long time ago; and how its leading exponents had become so clever that their designs looked just as well upside down as right side up, or sideways over. He proved his point by means of magic lantern pictures, which as everyone knows are more convincing than words, and sometimes even more convincing than buildings themselves. This round was declared a draw."

The AIA Octagon 2 (June 1930)

Simultaneously, Illinois Chapter membership declined and the Institute of Building Arts soon became a liability. In 1898 the Chapter left the building and exhibition space and moved to the Art Institute for their meetings. Unpaid dues and an apathetic membership hampered their effectiveness. In the past one of the more vocal Chicagoans active in the national organization, Dankmar Adler wrote to the AIA in 1898 of his discouragement with his profession:

"I cannot at this time say whether or not I shall be at the Convention at Washington....The Convention is going to be an Eastern Convention, a Convention of architects whose chief function is to collect big fees from their clients and then prove to them that they (the clients) ought to employ other people and pay them small fees to do a large portion of the work which a benighted Westerner like me thinks the architect is employed to do. The position of the big Eastern offices...is not at all conducive to raising the architect and his profession in the estimation of the public and cannot but prove injurious in the long run to the status of the architectural profession and its practitioners....Among the causes which have brought me to my present state of mind is the utter apathy of Western architects with the Institute and its affairs.[18]

Throughout the 1890s, Chicago's architects had continued to identify themselves as very different from what they believed to be their more conventional colleagues of the East Coast. The reform-minded architects of western regions seemed to believe that their criteria for redefining American architecture and for their profession were often in opposition with East Coast offices. By 1900, the usually optimistic Peter B. Wight wrote about the loss of one of his most respected colleagues, someone who represented some of the qualities that separated East Coast architects from Midwest architects:

"This week we lost by death our most representative man, Dankmar Adler. I have just returned from his funeral...With Root and Adler gone I fear that the profession in this city will lose some of the pre-eminence which it attained in 1890, when Architecture was I think a more progressive profession here than any where else, as I firmly believe...New reputations will doubtless be made and many old ones suffer. But soon the good effects of our license laws will begin to be felt more and more...[19]

In his letter Wight also mentioned the positive influence of the Club on the future of the profession. Although significantly different from the Chicago Chapter, the Chicago Architectural Club helped shape the architectural profession locally through its annual exhibitions and various educational goals. Peter B. Wight and some Chicago architects participated in club events, but more importantly, the city's draftsmen established ways to advance their skills and learn about the profession. While the Chicago Chapter AIA maintained strict professional standards for membership, the Club was far less restrictive. In contrast to the Chicago Chapter's steady decline in membership during the 1890s, the Chicago Architectural Club was prospering in the years around 1900.[20] Ironically, the Chicago AIA had helped establish architecture as a profession by means of the license law, yet it seemed that the Chapter had become less innovative. Interest had shifted elsewhere. Interest seemed to be shifting away from legislative issues and professional standards and toward new design ideas at the end of the century.

The Chapter's decline was brief, for many young reformers

1900-1917 Growth & A New Sense of Civic Responsibility

The Chapter's decline was brief, for many young reformers interested in the City Beautiful and parks movements would eventually become involved in the AIA, providing new vitality and civic spirit. By 1905-6 the Chapter was growing more active, probably due to the leadership of Irving K. Pond as its president. By 1911, the Chapter reached eighty-nine members, surpassing its high of the mid-1890s.[21] With the Chicago Architects Business Association relieving the Chapter of many duties, members turned with renewed commitment to civic plans. Beginning in 1904, the Chapter shared the club room at the Art Institute with the Municipal Art League of Chicago and the Chicago Society of Artists,[22] representing the increased interaction between the architects and civic groups in the early twentieth century. In 1905, Normand S. Patton introduced the subject of grouping Chicago's municipal buildings. Daniel H. Burnham chaired a committee to study municipal architecture and comprehensive planning. These efforts evolved to become the Commercial Club's highly influential *Plan of Chicago* by Burnham and Edward H. Bennett, endorsed by the Chicago Chapter and countless other municipal and civic groups.

At about this time, the Chapter appointed Elmer C. Jensen to chair the new Municipal Art Committee whose aim was to cooperate with the city to improve the design of public works. Committee member George W. Maher exhibited his work and spoke on the "Responsibility of the Architect to his Community" at the November 1911 Chapter meeting. As Maher later recalled in 1918,

> "At this time the architects as a class had not entered largely into Municipal work...there was also a peculiar skepticism regarding their ability to work constructively together and in harmony with other organizations. However, undaunted by the seeming hopelessness of the situation and fearless as the proverbial Don Quixote, they flung themselves strenuously into the fray determined to do something noteworthy for the public good and to assist in beautifying Chicago to their best ability."[23]

At a time when the business district was seriously congested, the committee quickly identified a noteworthy project for the public good: to improve the design of the proposed new city bridges over the Chicago River. "The problem was at once entered into with enthusiasm although the outlook at first was certainly discouraging. It required considerable effort on the part of the committee to convince the city authorities that the architects were really in earnest and intended to be of real constructive value in this...It also required the consent of the City Plan Commission so that we could properly cooperate with them."[24] Work began on the Monroe, Franklin-Orleans and Madison Street bridges. The Madison Street bridge, one of the main gateways from the train stations to the west, was the first to be studied and served as a model for future designs. In these projects, the committee collaborated with the Commissioners of Public Works, the City Engineering Department, and with Edward H. Bennett and William Parsons of the Chicago Plan Commission. The committee continued to work on the designs for bridges at LaSalle, 12th Street, and Michigan Avenue through the 1920s. The Chapter's contribution to these important public works projects is acknowledged on several Chicago River bridge commemorative plaques.

While increasing activity in the public sphere, the Chapter also developed a stronger organizational coherence . In November 1910, it moved into a newly renovated club room at the Art Institute, which it continued to share with other organizations for the next fourteen years.[25] The members began to collect portraits for a "gallery of architects" in 1913, beginning with a portrait of Peter B. Wight. Even twenty to thirty years later, members recalled the memorable meeting of June 1915 at the Cliff Dwellers Club, when portraits of Daniel Burnham and Solon S. Beman were unveiled. The presidents of the AIA and the Art Institute, prominent artists, and others with a public spirit were guests as Charles Wacker and Louis H. Sullivan presented the Burnham and Beman portraits. By the time the United States entered World War I, the Illinois Chapter numbered 156 and a sound basis for involvement in civic affairs was established.

1917-1929: Civic Affairs and Business Success

The 1920s saw the largest building boom in Chicago since the 1880s, as well as a strong sense of social reform and civic responsibility. The Chapter participated in local civic affairs and agitated for zoning regulation. The war years were turbulent and busy ones for the organization. Work with the Municipal Art Committee continued under Chapter President Maher's guidance during and after the war.

In these rapidly changing times there was general dissatisfaction with the conservatism of the national AIA. The vast majority of architects did not belong to the AIA,[26] which some felt was due to its aloof and aristocratic attitude. Charles Hammond went so far as to encourage a Federation of State Societies, feeling that organizational competition would enliven the Institute. In 1918, President Maher and Secretary Henry Holsman were sole representatives to the AIA Convention, charged by the chapter with changing the AIA Code of Ethics regarding its conservative position on advertising.[27] The conflict revolved around the AIA's

Portrait of Dankmar Adler, by Oskar Gross, oil on canvas, 1916. Adler served as AIA Chicago President 1897-98. (Photograph courtesy of Chicago Historical Society: 1943.42)

Portrait of Irving K. Pond and Allen Bartlet Pond, by Ralph Clarkson, oil on canvas, undated. Irving K. Pond served as AIA Chicago President 1905-06. (Photograph courtesy of Chicago Historical Society: 1943.52)

Presidents	Birthdates	Years in Office
Harry B. Wheelock FAIA	(1861-1934)	1925-27
John C. Bollenbacher FAIA (	1884-1939)	1927-29
Howard L. Cheney FAIA	(1889-1969)	1929-31
Clarence W. Farrier	(Dates unknown)	1931-33
Eugene H. Klaber FAIA	(1883-1971)	1933
Earl H. Reed, Jr. FAIA	(1884-1968)	1933-34
Emery S. Hall FAIA	(1869-1939)	1934-36
John O. Merrill FAIA	(1896-1975)	1936-38
Elmer C. Roberts	(1896-1981)	1938-40
Jerrold Loebl FAIA	(1899-1978)	1940-42
Nathaniel A. Owings FAIA	(1903-1984)	1942-43
Alfred P. Shaw FAIA	(1895-1970)	1943-45
Paul Gerhardt, Jr. FAIA	(1899-1966)	1945-47
John S. Cromelin FAIA	(1895-1957)	1947-48
Norman J. Schlossman FAIA	(1901-1990)	1948-50
L. Morgan Yost FAIA	(1908-1992)	1950-52
Philip Will, Jr. FAIA	(1906-1985)	1952-54
Alfred S. Alschuler, Jr. FAIA	(1911-)	1954-55

position that an architect's name on a building under construction was a form of advertising and should not be allowed. Once again, practical Midwestern attitudes conflicted with those from East Coast cities. Again, the westerners prevailed, and the editor of *The American Architect* reported afterwards that "the past conservatism, closely allied with old-fogyism, had seen its day, and that there were in the saddle a lot of men who fully realized the work cut out for them and knew just how to set about it....the men of the Middle West, whose broad vision and practical views were a very important feature in all the convention proceedings."[28]

The 1919 Annual Convention saw an even more active Illinois Chapter, armed with resolutions on architectural education and state societies. Earlier they had influenced the AIA to allow members to do construction work on a cost plus fee system and still retain their professional standing.[29] Later the head of the National Committee on Education, George Nimmons proposed a college course in architecture, an idea which originated in a lecture he delivered to the Association of American Colleges. He obtained the AIA's support to work with this group to plan the course. From these efforts, they published a college textbook. Irving K. Pond wrote later that it was "one of the most constructive and inspiring [conventions] that it had ever been his privilege to attend."[30] In 1921 the Illinois delegation came with seven resolutions including uniform registration laws and building codes and revisions to the AIA Schedule of Charges and the Canon of Ethics.[31]

Immediately after the war, architects faced several slow years. By early 1921, the economic slowdown resulted in lockouts and strikes in all of the building trades. Graft and restraint of trade were common problems that prompted Chapter efforts to combat these troubles. An important issue in its day, the conflict surrounding wage scales attracted the public's interest. Arbitration finally resulted in the Landis Award, named for the presiding judge. Judge Landis had received advice from the Chapter in his considerations of a just wage scale. The AIA afterwards supported the Citizens Committee to Enforce the Landis Award, and continued to take an active interest in issues of labor and the building trades well into the 1920s.

In 1922 labor unrest and high costs diminished enough to set off a burst of building activity. Renamed the Chicago Chapter in 1923 when the new Central Illinois Chapter was founded, the Chapter began publishing a monthly newsletter written and edited by former Chapter president Henry K. Holsman. Called *The Leaflet*, the monthly publication ran until 1929, taking as its motto "To Make the Profession of Ever-increasing Service to Society."

Henry Holsman had identified "service" as the goal of the architectural profession in his June 1919 inaugural speech. Chaired by George W. Maher, the renamed Municipal Art and Town Planning Committee in 1919 appointed subcommittees in the following areas: improvement of Chicago bridges, the Palace of the Fine Arts (called the Field Museum then), proposed lakefront improvement, North Michigan Avenue improvements, and a comprehensive zoning law.[32] They made recommendations on issues affecting the Chicago Plan and served as a watchdog guarding against encroachments on it.

Although supported by most of the city's civic and technical groups, public effort to establish a comprehensive zoning law was a long and difficult battle. Agitation began in Chicago during the early 1910s and several attempts to pass a zoning bill in the Legislature failed, but legislation (known as the Glacken Enabling Act) was eventually approved in March of 1919. Following this achievement, Chicago groups set about to draft an appropriate zoning ordinance. Chair of the Chapter Zoning Subcommittee, Allen B. Pond submitted a report to the City Council and offered the service of the Chapter and the AIA Archives for drafting the new law. Charles Hammond, Chapter past-president and current president of the Illinois Society of Architects, was the architectural representative on a tour of cities with city officials to study the strengths of other planning laws. The Citizens' Zoning Plan Conference represented 77 organizations and it listened to papers by many planning experts and architects, including Chapter members Edward H. Bennett and Howard Van Doren Shaw. In February 1920, the city passed an ordinance creating the Chicago Zoning Commission, and the mayor appointed the Commission with Bennett as Director of Zoning. The Commission drafted the zoning ordinance which passed in April 1923. Allen B. Pond, was appointed Chairman of the Zoning Board of Appeals.

The most highly publicized cause undertaken by the Chapter in the 1920s was the restoration of the Palace of the Fine Arts Building, left standing after the 1893 World's Columbian Exposition (now the Museum of Science and Industry). The story began at the September 1919 Illinois Chapter meeting, where sculptor and honorary AIA member Lorado Taft suggested that the building should be preserved and then used to hold sculptural and architectural models. Recently abandoned by the Field Museum of Natural History, the Exposition's last remaining building was threatened with demolition. The Chicago Chapter and the Illinois Society of Architects financed a detailed estimate completed in 1921 by members of the Municipal Art Committee and submitted to the South Park Commissioners. In the meantime, they enlisted civic organizations and the press. The Second District Illinois Federation of Women's Clubs raised $5,000, which was donated to the AIA for restoration of the building's northwest corner. They hoped that the improvement would show the feasibility of restoration and enlist more public support. The Chapter then arranged for the gala dinner of the 1922 AIA Convention to be held in the rotunda of the museum building. The dinner drew national attention to the building's fate, while also boosting local press and civic effort. Eventually Graham, Anderson, Probst and White drew plans for restoration in 1926, which the chapter critiqued. In 1926-27 Mr. Julius Rosenwald gave $3,000,000 to restore the building for use as an industrial museum. In 1929 after a decade of involvement, Holsman wrote: "That activity has probably done more than any other to make a place for the Chapter among the leading civic organizations or to make the citizens conscious of the value of architects in the community."[33]

A New Home

When a new director took over the Art Institute in the early 1920s, relations between the Institute and the architectural societies declined. Storage privileges were eliminated and in 1924 the Chapter was asked to remove its portrait collection and vacate the club rooms. In the spring, a casual discussion between members of the Illinois Society of Architects and the Chicago Chapter resulted in a major step for both societies. President of the Chicago Chapter, Alfred Granger described in an informal cocktail conversation how much he regretted that the architectural profession in Chicago was financially unable to own and operate its own club building. Someone suggested that "the well-known Glessner house ... would be an ideal building to house the architectural profession in Chicago."[34] Following several coctails, it is reported that ISA President Charles Fox suggested to Granger that the architects "ask Mr. Glessner to provide in his will that the architects should have the first opportunity to purchase his house." A few days later, Alfred Granger convinced his friend Mr. Glessner to preserve his important home. Glessner promised to deed his home to the Chicago Chapter upon his death on the condition that the architects occupy the Kimball mansion until he died, thus protecting him from undesirable neighbors. Since none of the organizations could purchase the Kimball property outright, the Architects' Realty Trust was created to do so. The Trust in turn leased the home to the newly formed Architects Club of Chicago, the Chicago Chapter, ISA, and the Chicago Architectural Club. The holders of investment certificates formed the proprietary membership of the Architects Club of Chicago. Regular members paid a $100 initiation fee and yearly dues. The Kimball property was purchased for $82,000. A membership drive sought to recruit representatives of contracting and building material organizations, in addition to architects, with the hope that a common meeting place would provide greater unity and understanding among the building and architectural interests. While all the societies shared the privileges of the Kimball House, title to the Glessner house would go to the Chicago Chapter AIA upon Mr. Glessner's death.

The Chapter moved with its portrait collection to a temporary room at the University Club until arrangements with the Realty Trust were complete. On May 12, 1925, the Chicago Chapter met for the first time in the Kimball House. The Chicago Architectural Sketch Club Atelier set up its studio over the Kimball garage, and all three societies held their monthly meetings in the Club. This marks the high point of cooperation among the various architectural societies in Chicago, which shared many of the same members. The Club was quite successful for several years. Strained relations with the Art Institute were finally broken in 1929 when the Architectural Exhibition League began to hold its exhibits at the Arts Club instead of at the Institute.[35] The Chapter grew less active as intense speculation and building climaxed in the late 1920s. The Chicago Chapter AIA tried to capitalize on the economic boom with an ambitious scheme to build an Architects Office Building on LaSalle Street. A committee drew up a detailed report, but nothing ever materialized. The Municipal Arts Committee reported little activity in 1927. As was the pattern in the past, an increase in prosperity saw a corresponding decrease in the activities of the professional organizations.

1929-1945: Depression And War

Portrait of Dwight H. Perkins, by Henry Salem Hubbell, oil on canvas, ca. 1920. Perkins served as AIA Chicago President 1907-09. (Photograph courtesy of Chicago Historical Society: 1943.55)

Presidents	Birthdates	Years in Office
Samuel A. Lichtmann FAIA	(1898-1977)	1955-57
John R. Fugard Jr. FAIA	(1912-1981)	1957-59
William J. Bachman FAIA	(1914-1989)	1959-61
R. Rea Esgar FAIA	(1905-1966)	1961-63
Jack Train FAIA	(1922-)	1963-64
Walter H. Sobel FAIA	(1913-)	1965
Paul D. McCurry FAIA	(1903 -1991)	1966
D. Coder Taylor FAIA	(1913-)	1967
Morton Hartman FAIA	(1923-)	1968
Spencer B. Cone FAIA	(1910-)	1969
Richard M. Bennett FAIA	(1907-)	1970
M. David Dubin FAIA	(1927-)	1971
William E. Dunlap FAIA	(1922-1973)	1972
Carter H. Manny, Jr. FAIA	(1918-)	1973
Bruno P. Conterato FAIA	(1920-)	1974
Harry M. Weese FAIA	(1915-)	1975
H. Thurber Stowell, Jr. FAIA	(1920-)	1976
John A. Holabird, Jr. FAIA	(1920-)	1977
Raymond C. Ovresat FAIA	(1926-)	1978
Clarence Krusinski	(1940-)	1979
Gertrude Lempp Kerbis FAIA	(1926-)	1980
Richard B. Cook FAIA	(1937-)	1981
Donald J. Hackl FAIA	(1934-)	1982
Charles W. Brubaker FAIA	(1926-)	1983
Thomas J. Eyerman FAIA	(1939-)	1984
Norman R. DeHaan FAIA	(1927-1990)	1985-86
Edward K. Uhlir FAIA	(1944-)	1986-87
Cynthia Weese FAIA	(1940-)	1987-88
Frank Heitzman AIA	(1946-)	1988-89
Steven F. Weiss AIA	(1949-)	1989-90
Sherwin J. Braun AIA	(1936-)	1990-91
Leonard A. Peterson AIA	(1937-)	1991-92
Linda Searl AIA	(1947-)	1992-93
John H. Nelson AIA	(1945-)	1993-94

The October 1929 issue of the *Illinois Society of Architects Monthly Bulletin* described the previous year as a successful one for the Architects Club of Chicago. The architectural societies, the Real Estate Board, and the Building Managers Association were successful in appealing a recent zoning amendment which increased the heights of buildings. The business report described a decrease in building from the previous year, part of a nation-wide slump, but the general tone was positive. Shortly before the crash of 1929, the Chapter wished to boost the public image of the architect through use of the media. Arthur Woltersdorf, the Chairman of the Committee on Public Information, arranged to have articles on architecture printed in the Sunday edition of the *Chicago Herald & Examiner* for sixteen weeks, beginning September 29. Prominent Chicago architects such as John A. Holabird wrote about the skyscraper, and Irving K. Pond contributed his important essay "Toward an American Architecture." Eventually, Woltersdorf compiled these writings in a book entitled *Living Architecture*, published in 1930. Woltersdorf's involvement in publicity had begun earlier in the 1920s, when his committee had thirty articles published in the Sunday *Tribune* and the *Herald & Examiner* during 1923-4. The first topic in the series was Louis H. Sullivan's *Autobiography of an Idea*. Subsequent articles included book reviews, historical articles, competitions, and housing issues. The Public Information Committee continued its media campaign into the 1930s, but *Tribune* articles written by Chapter members in 1930 focused more on small scale issues, reflecting the severe slump in construction in the first two or three years of the decade. The Chapter cut expenses, eliminated the Sketch Club traveling scholarship, and ceased publication of *The Leaflet*.

By late 1933, new government agencies provided work for architects. At the national level, the Historic American Buildings Survey (HABS) employed scores of draftsmen. In Chicago, Chapter president Earl H. Reed, Jr., an expert in Greek Revival architecture in Illinois, was appointed District officer in northern Illinois for HABS.[36] Government work also drew many of the Chapter's more experienced architects, such as President Eugene Klaber, to Washington. Although much of the effort during the Depression was directed toward unemployment and government work, the Chapter also continued to host presentations on topics of architectural interest. The tradition of monthly business meetings combined with cocktails, dinner and guest speakers continued. Meetings were often held with the Illinois Society of Architects. Discussions of Modernism became more common before the 1933 Century of Progress Exposition. A memorable highlight at this time was Le Corbusier's first visit to the United States. On November 27, 1935, a crowd listened to Le Corbusier speak at the Stevens Hotel, following a dinner sponsored by the city's numerous architectural groups. Addressing his audience in French, he spoke about urbanism, all the while drawing on ten foot long sheets of paper with colored crayons. Afterward he showed slides and "moving pictures" of his work.[37]

The building business continued to slump, and the Chapter continued to shrink. President Merrill made a plea for new membership and continued the Public Information Committee in 1936. Architects faced encroachment on their profession, particularly from residential builders. At this low point in its fortunes, the Chapter was faced with the prospect of taking over the Glessner House after Mr. Glessner's death. By April 1937 the Club found it necessary either to assume the Glessner property or release it to an attorney. The Executive Committee was finally authorized to give up the Glessner House gift, since the Chapter could not assume the renovation or maintenance costs. The Kimball House, vacated in February 1939 and left to the Realty Trust, was eventually rented and then sold to a private school in 1943.

During the Depression, the Chapter attempted to help the younger unemployed draftsmen. The annual architects' ball began to raise money to finance an atelier for the education of architectural draftsmen. This so-called "Chicago School of Architecture" was organized and operated by the Chicago Chapter and directed by architect Paul Schweikher in 1939. Each student was required to be a Junior Associate member of the Chicago Chapter, which encouraged young architects to participate in AIA activities.[38]

By 1940, a younger generation of architects had replaced older leadership and the Chapter's goals changed. The architectural societies went their separate ways. The Architectural Club found space at the Merchandise Mart, the ISA met in the Empire room of the Piccadilly Restaurant at Michigan and Van Buren, and the Chicago Chapter alternated between the Tavern Club and the Normandy House on Tower Court. In 1941, the AIA and ISA entered negotiations with the Skyline Club in the Bell Building for permanent headquarters, but the parties did not reach an acceptable agreement. The Chapter portrait collection, in storage since its removal from the Kimball House, was donated to the Chicago Historical Society in 1943, symbolically cutting Chapter ties with the past.

1945-1960: New Directions, Growing Pains

From 1920 to 1943, membership in the Chicago Chapter had hovered above 200, dropping to a low of 175 in 1937. But between 1943 and 1953, membership more than doubled and the organization's interests changed. With the return of war veterans in 1946, the Chapter began to issue a monthly *Bulletin*. Meetings were held regularly on the first Tuesday of each month, at the Builders' Club, where members discussed housing, the Chicago Plan Commission, building codes, education, the profession, and a new state organization for architects. The Illinois Architects Association (now the AIA Illinois), a council of Illinois chapters of the American Institute of Architects, met for the first time in September, 1946. Charles Hammond was its first president. Two months later its name was changed to the Architects Association of Illinois, after the Illinois Society of Archi-

tects objected to the similarity of names. Since the move from the Kimball house in 1939, Chicago's architectural societies drifted apart and, after forty-five years of close association, the Chapter and the Illinois Society gradually fell out of contact.

The late 1940s and early 1950s were active years for the Chicago Chapter AIA and the architectural profession. A sense of camaraderie returned. Organized by Harry Weese, popular "inspection tours" of members' buildings brought Chicago's architects together to discuss contemporary architecture. To meet the professional needs of younger members, the Chapter developed a series of extension courses with the University of Illinois at Navy Pier and supported student chapters. Activity at the national AIA level resulted in the first National AIA Honor Awards Program in 1949; Perkins and Will won the Award of Merit that year. Supported by John W. Root, Jr., the Chapter agitated for a national AIA advertising campaign and public relations throughout the 1950s.

Locally, the Chapter worked toward the same ends. In 1949 it used the new medium of television to broadcast a single show, "What the Architect Does." Later that year the "Architect-Client Relationship Clinics" were initiated at the Cliff Dwellers Club when Jerrold Loebl presented "How to Get a Client." The series was well attended. In 1953, as the profession became more complicated, the Chapter hired an outside public relations consultant and later a Director of Public Relations.

In the January 1951 *Bulletin,* President L. Morgan Yost wrote, "What are we to do with this year of 1951 which seems to promise only restrictions, shortages, allocations, discouragement and difficulties?" Despite a lack of building activity, the Chapter was busy examining activities outside the traditional realm of architecture, such as problems of neighborhood conservation and planning. The newly formed Civic Affairs Committee pursued new goals along with conventional ones like zoning. Its chairman was Harry Weese, followed by William Deknatel and John W. Root, Jr. By 1954 the committee had changed its name to the Planning Committee, reflecting a new emphasis in urban development. Subcommittees addressed the various problems associated with new suburban expansion, and urban blight.[39] Frustrated by city bureaucracies, Chapter members found they were "too few in number to raise a concerted voice in behalf of sound planning and to exercise the influence commensurate with our professional know-how."[40]

In 1954, the Chapter tried to exert its influence in the controversial project for a convention hall. Objecting to the proposed lakefront site for its great distance from and inaccessibility to the businesses and hotels of the central business district, the Chapter Committee on the Convention Center released its study on proposed alternative sites. To promote redevelopment and to support downtown businesses, the Chapter proposed three alternative sites, one slightly south of the Loop, one just north of the Chicago River, and the third on Illinois Central Railroad air rights east of Michigan Avenue, north of Randolph. The study, complete with massing models and drawings, was formally submitted to Paul Gerhardt, Jr., City Architect. Despite their arguments, the lakefront site was selected for the future McCormick Place.

1926

At the May national AIA convention in New York, George C. Nimmons presented a paper just before a discussion about American architecture and modern art. An observer described some of these remarks:

"...but the most interesting [event] was the resolution proposed by Mr. George C. Nimmons to convict certain modern artists of heresy and to proclaim to the world that henceforth they should be branded and treated as outcasts. Novel theories have ever been terrifying to mankind and primitive instinct prompts drastic measures of self defense against the unfamiliar... But society has become so infected and weakened by modernism that its present manner is to ostracize or ignore."

The resolution was tabled.

Journal of the American Institute of Architects 14 no 6 (June 1926)

Following the first AIA Gold Medal in 1907, seven architects practicing in Chicago have been awarded this honor:

Howard Van Doren Shaw	**1927**
Louis H. Sullivan	**1944**
Frank Lloyd Wright	**1949**
Louis Skidmore	**1957**
John W. Root, Jr.	**1958**
Ludwig Mies van der Rohe	**1960**
Nathaniel Owings	**1983**

In 1951, the Chapter opened a small office in the Monadnock Building, its first permanent space since leaving the Kimball House. This year, the Board also hired its first full-time employee. Meetings were held in other locations, including the Western Society of Engineers club room, the Swedish Club, and the Blackstone Hotel. In 1953, the Chapter rewrote its bylaws to reflect the new goals of a much larger organization. President Will wrote that the bylaws changes brought mixed results in 1953. In a Chapter *Bulletin* members were asked to address what was wrong with the AIA. Beset by the inherent difficulties of a larger organization, the Chapter was faulted because it was run by members of larger offices, because it failed to address smaller architectural firms, and because older members failed to provide leadership for the profession.

The Chapter continued to grow throughout the mid 1950s, showing an 80% growth in membership between 1955 and 1957. The Chicago Chapter was now the largest chapter in the country after California. The organization moved into new larger space in the LaSalle & Wacker Building, and held monthly exhibits of local artists' work in the Chapter offices. Though the leadership felt that architects were gaining respect and making progress in civic and professional affairs, lack of participation continued to be a problem.

In September 1957 the first issue of a new *Inland Architect* was published by the Chicago Chapter AIA to replace the *Bulletin*, with Raymond C. Ovresat as editor. The first issue applauded the passing of the Illinois Architecture Act after years of AIA efforts, and described "Chicago Dynamic Week." Focusing on architecture, the week of October 27 highlighted workshops, seminars, lectures, and tours. The week ended with an interview with Frank Lloyd Wright and Carl Sandburg, hosted by Alistair Cooke. The following year, the Chapter helped to form the Women's Architectural League, primarily a group of architects' wives dedicated to supporting the profession and educating the public. A few years later, the Chapter encouraged the new Association of Architectural Secretaries, another group supporting the profession. The next decade would see an increase in public awareness and support of architecture.

1960-1980: Broadening The Profession

In the 1960s and 1970s, the Chicago Chapter shared in a general diversification of the profession, whether through extended architectural services, the image of the profession, or the membership of the profession. The preservation movement was an important development of the 1950s, as architects and other groups developed a new attitude toward historic architecture which had a long-lasting impact on the city and on the public view of architecture. Before this time, little had been done by the AIA to document or preserve Chicago's architecture. An isolated early example was the effort of Thomas E. Tallmadge and the Illinois Chapter Historical Committee to save the old Water Tower in 1918. In the late 1920s and early 1930s, the Materials and Methods Committee documented the wrecking of highly important and historic structures such as the Home Insurance and Tacoma Buildings. Rather than saving these famous structures, the committee

AIA Offices in the U. S. Gypsum Building, 1965. (Photo by Hedrich-Blessing. Photograph courtesy of AIA Chicago)

members were only interested in documenting the structural systems of the early Chicago School. This documentation strategy was supported by HABS programs of the 1930s and later by the Architectural Microfilming Project, conducted by the Art Institute's Burnham Library beginning in 1950. This project was created by several architects and engineers, including Chapter past-presidents Earl Reed, Jr. and Elmer C. Jensen.[41]

As chair of the National AIA Committee on Preservation in the early 1950s, Earl Reed, Jr. encouraged the formation of local AIA preservation committees. The Chapter's Committee on Preservation of Historic Buildings, later called the Historic Resources Committee, was created in 1952. Many members devoted time to inventorying historically significant structures, but they found it difficult to raise interest in public and private groups. As the committee reported in 1954: "This task is particularly difficult at this time when so much of our urban areas are in a state of decay and the demand for funds for redevelopment is so great."[42] In a 1957 hearing, John W. Root, Jr., John Fugard, Earl H. Reed, Samuel Lichtmann, George Keck, and Charles Dornbusch were among the architects who spoke in favor of the Commission on Chicago Landmarks.

Although lost, the preservation battle to save Louis H. Sullivan's Stock Exchange Building in 1970 rallied the city and the Chapter and established the landmark preservation movement. Most efforts until this time had been focused on documentation. The prevailing attitude among architects was that architects should not oppose developers. It was not until the Stock Exchange that the Chapter took a strong stand.[43] In February 1970, with Sullivan's famous building scheduled for demolition that summer, Chapter president Richard Bennett appeared at a public hearing before the Landmarks Commission to propose a change in the zoning ordinance which the Chapter had developed. By April they had met with representatives of the Metropolitan Housing and Planning Commission which was studying legislation built around the Chapter's proposal for transferring floor area rights. In February 1971, the office of Harry Weese & Associates gave grant money to the Chapter Foundation to have John Costonis of the Univerity of Illinois Law School study this Development Rights Transfer Proposal for landmark buildings. The battle was finally lost, but both architects and laymen left with a heightened awareness of important preservation and development issues.

Preservation gave the profession a higher public profile, but the Chapter was involved with other issues as well, including its successful efforts to prevent the proposed Crosstown Expressway, a twenty-two mile elevated roadway planned for construction in 1966. Chicago Chapter president Paul McCurry spoke out against the expressway before the Chicago Plan Commission, City Club of Chicago, many neighborhood groups, and at a highly publicized press conference. As Paul Gapp, then Executive Director of the Chicago Chapter wrote, "Reporters present, particularly those experienced in urban affairs coverage, expressed pleasure over the direct and forceful language of Mr. McCurry's statement....The Crosstown Expressway in its proposed form would be a costly, ugly and inefficient blot on the cityscape — a monument to poor planning....If an elevated Crosstown Expressway is built, it will become Chicago's biggest, ugliest and perhaps most long-lived landmark."[44] The publicity stirred protest from the communities and the Federal Bureau of Public Roads asked for a new study of the Crosstown and other urban roadways.

In order to boost its professional image, the Chapter and the Illinois Council (formerly the Architectural Association of Illinois) moved into new offices in the USG Building in 1965. By 1968, *Inland Architect* was in financial trouble and it was reorganized as the Inland Architect Corporation and improved.[45] The Chapter focused its energy on the upcoming 1969 AIA Convention in Chicago. Unfortunately, due to unexpected backlash from the 1968 Democratic Convention, fewer people attended than had been anticipated, leaving the Chapter in debt for nearly a decade.

When the USG lease expired in 1971, one year after the loss of the Stock Exchange, the Chapter had another opportunity to occupy the Glessner House, more than thirty years after it had relinquished the Glessner deed. The Glessner House had passed to the Armour Institute of Technology in 1938, and was sold twenty years later to the Graphic Arts Technical Foundation. When it was again on the market in 1965, concern over its fate led to a search for an organization which would preserve the house. Finally, in March 1966, a group of interested people formed the Chicago School of Architecture Foundation. Chicago Chapter members Harry and Ben Weese, among others, had been actively involved with the preservation efforts and they undertook the fundraising. Two months later, enough pledges were received from the architectural community (in addition to a large contribution by Philip Johnson) to make an offer. Ben Weese was named Chairman of the Board of Trustees, Wilbert R. Hasbrouck the President, and several Chapter members sat on the Board. Chapter Past-President L. Morgan Yost, a historian of Chicago architecture, took the job of Executive Director. The Chicago Chapter and the Illinois Council moved into the Glessner House in August, 1971.

In 1976 the Illinois Council (formerly the Illinois Association of Architects) decided to become a separate entity, a difficult administrative proposition after several years of shared resources. After occupying separate offices in the Glessner House for a year, the Illinois Council moved to Springfield, while the Chicago Chapter moved in 1977 to the recently created ArchiCenter at 111 South Dearborn, the Santa Fe Building, and then to the Monadnock Building in 1981.

Meanwhile, the social protest and community action of the 1960s had inspired an era of intense community involvement to combat poverty and urban blight. In 1968 the Chapter initiated a Neighborhood Design Center program which provided volunteer professional advice and assistance for citizens seeking to improve their neighborhoods. The Uptown Design Center was cited by the national AiA as a model organization, and in 1971 the center became an accredited Drafting School under the direction of AIA members. The Chicago Architectural Assistance Center was started in 1974 with the Legal Assistance Foundation of Chicago.

The late 1960s and 1970s witnessed a diversification of the profession. Increasing numbers of minorities and women entered the profession and joined the Chapter, which up until this time had been almost exclusively white and male. In 1965 Andrew Heard was the first African-American to join the Chapter Board. In response to Whitney Young's challenge at the 1968 National AIA Convention, the Chapter actively encouraged minority involvement. At the January meeting in 1969, the Black Architects Collaborative presented a program called "Black Communities and Their Architects." There had been a handful of women members in the Chicago Chapter since Elizabeth Kimball Nedved became its first female member in 1927,[46] but not until the 1970s were there substantial numbers. In 1970 Gertrude Lempp Kerbis became the first woman from the Chicago Chapter to be made a Fellow of the AIA, and only the tenth nationally. Kerbis became the first female president of the Chapter in 1980.

Summing Up

After surviving the recession and debt of the 1970s, the Chapter worked to re-establish itself as a vital force in the 1980s. The Chapter lobbied in the late 1970s for increased support from some of the larger Chicago firms which had not been active for some time. It held Saturday morning meetings to discuss plans for the World's Fair in the late 1970s. These meetings were attended by many prominent architects. Even after the Commercial Club took over the project, the enthusiasm carried over to a new interest in urban planning. The local Design Committee and Interiors Committee were new in 1980, but through the 1980s much of the energy in design-related issues shifted to the new Chicago Architectural Club.

Through the recession of the 1970s and the 1980s, the AIA saw a gradual erosion of its Code of Ethics established in 1909. A decade of pressure from within the AIA and, beginning in 1972, pressure from the Justice Department, saw the gradual demise of a strict code of ethics. As the 1980s expanded economically, the profession was unfettered by professional restrictions on competition, advertising, or supplanting of another architect. Making free sketches, now commonplace, was one of the last tenets to go.

The boom of the 1980s was followed by the recession of the 1990s. Ironically, neighborhood redevelopment and scattered site housing, ideas previously studied by the Chapter Planning and Housing Committees during the early 1970s are only now taking form. Technology, computers, and new methods of practice are blurring the traditional boundaries of architecture. As we reach the 100th Anniversary of the Illinois licensing law, new challenges will alter the profession and its practice.

It is interesting to note in light of recent criticism of the national AIA and recurring complaints of low participation that this has all happened before. Periods of inactivity and dissatisfaction have alternated with bursts of enthusiasm typically focused on a particular cause and often dependent upon economic conditions. Worthy causes have demanded patience and constant vigilance to see results. The pendulum has swung from design to business more than once. Since World War II, the sudden growth of the Chapter and the onslaught of information and technology have made internal communication and fragmentation frequent problems. But tenacity, outspokenness, and energetic leadership have, over the years, characterized the highlights of the Chicago Chapter's professional activity.

Kathleen Nagle, AIA is a praticing architect in Chicago with Holabird and Root. In addition to serving as an AIA Illinois Delegate, Ms. Nagle served this year on the jury for the Chicago Award.

The Chapter would like to thank the Graham Foundation for Advanced Studies in the Fine Arts for its generous support. Thanks also go to Tony Wrenn, archivist for the AIA, for helping to locate many interesting traces of the Chapter's past, and also to Alice Sinkevitch and Laurie McGovern Petersen for their research assistance.

Endnotes

1. Chicago's architects had independently recognized the need for organization prior to the formation of the AIA and a dozen or so years before founding a chapter. In John Van Osdel's books of account for 1856 there is an undated professional agreement, including enumeration of fees, signed by eleven men - the major architects in pre-fire Chicago. This was only twelve years after Van Osdel set up practice as the first architect in the city, and underscores the difficulties encountered in trying to establish the profession. For more information see Frank A. Randall, *History of the Development of Building Construction in Chicago* (Chicago: University of Chicago Press, 1949), p. 24.

2. For more on Jenney, see Theodore Turak, *William Le Baron Jenney: A Pioneer of Modern Architecture* (Ann Arbor: UMI Research Press), p. 115.

3. Chicago Chapter of the American Institute of Architects, *Proceedings of the Fifth Annual Convention* (1871)

4. *The Leaflet* no. 52 (April 1929), p.1.

5. *The Leaflet* no. 52 (April 1929), p. 1.

6. *The Leaflet* no. 11 (January 1924), p. 3.

7. Chicago Chapter of the American Institute of Architects, *Proceedings of the Seventh Annual Convention* (1873). Address by Peter B. Wight

8. Chicago Chapter of The American Institute of Architects, *Proceedings of the Ninth Annual Convention* (1875)

9. See article by Robert McLean. *Illinois Society of Architects Monthly Bulletin* 2 no. 6 (December 1917), p. 1. In 1883, the Chapter was represented solely by its Secretary.

10. *The Leaflet* no.14 (April 1924), p. 3.

11. *Inland Architect* 3 no. 4 (May 1884), p. 47

12. *The Leaflet* no. 17 (October 1924), p. 3. Members included John Wellborn Root, Henry Ives Cobb, L. D. Cleveland, Normand S. Patton, William W. Clay, O. L. Wheelock, Daniel H. Burnham, L. Gustav Hallberg, William Holabird, Samuel A. Treat, Stephen V. Shipman, William Le Baron Jenney, Louis H. Sullivan, Dankmar Adler, John Addison, and others. For more, see Inland Architect 4 no. 4 (November 1884), p. 4.

13. Chicago Chapter of The American Institute of Architects, *Proceedings of the Twenty-Second Annual Convention* (1888), p. 26.

14. *The Leaflet* no. 23 (May 1924), p. 3.

15. *The Leaflet* no. 33 (December 1926), p. 3.

16. *Illinois Society of Architects Monthly Bulletin* 7 no. 1 (July 1922), p. 8. The bill was first introduced into the Illinois State Legislature and piloted through the House by Representative Northnagel, a Chicago architect.

17. Ibid., p. 8.

18. Letter from Dankmar Adler to Mr. Stone of the AIA, October 4, 1898, from the AIA Archives.

19. Letter from Peter B. Wight to Glenn Brown, Secretary of the AIA, April 18, 1900, from the AIA Archives.

20. While the Chapter membership numbered about forty in 1900, the Architectural Club was much larger with 150 draftsmen and architects. The Chicago Architectural Club, renamed in 1893-94, was originally called the Chicago Architectural Sketch Club.

21. In 1909 the Chapter included part of Northern Indiana. In 1918 it annexed all of Indiana with its five AIA members. Indiana established its own chapter in 1923.

22. Illinois Chapter Report, 1905, from the AIA Archives.

23. See article by George W. Maher in *Illinois Society of Architects Monthly Bulletin* 2 no. 9 (March, 1918), p. 3.

24. Ibid., p. 3.

25. The Club Room was to be located at the north end of the main building on the basement floor. Illinois Chapter Report, 1910, from the AIA Archives.

26. There were 10-15,000 unaffiliated architects in the country around 1920 and only 1,500 in the AIA. In Chicago there were 772 licensed architects, exclusive of the 132 AIA members. Many young architects were out of work. (AIA Archives, letter from Box 99s)

27. The AIA Code of Ethics was written in 1909.

28. *The Leaflet* no. 52 (April 1929), p. 5..

29. *Journal of the American Institute of Architects* 7 no. 3, (March 1919), p. 157.

30. *Illinois Society of Architects Bulletin* 3 no. 11 (May 1919), p. 1.

31. *Journal of the American Institute of Architects* 9 no.7, (July 1921), pp. 250-1. A Boston observer wrote: "...one must note with admiration the advanced methods of the Illinois Chapter. This year the regular orators of this delegation were constantly relieved by a group of young men, in the flower of their youth, who took the floor whenever one of the veterans showed signs of falling below the average output of words per minute. It was an inspiring example of team-play, and it suggested that the members of this delegation might practice at the bar as well as at the drawing-board."

32. Committee members were Daniel H. Burnham, Elmer C. Jensen, Alfred Granger, Francis Puckey, Martin Roche, Richard E. Schmidt, Howard Van Doren Shaw, and Thomas E. Tallmadge.

33. *The Leaflet* no. 52 (April 1929), p. 7.

34. *Illinois Society of Architects Bulletin* (Dec 1924), as reprinted in Vol. 1, No.1 (January 1925) of Chicago Architects Club Bulletin.

35. The Architectural Exhibition League was formed in 1924 with a board of directors of three each from the Illinois Society of Architects, the Chicago Chapter AIA and the Sketch Club.

36. *Illinois Society of Architects Bulletin* 18 (Dec/Jan 1933-34), pp. 6-7.

37. *Illinois Society of Architects. Bulletin* 20 (Dec/Jan 1935-36), pp. 1-2. The Chicago Chapter AIA and the Illinois Society of Architects financed his visit to Chicago. He gave two additional talks, one to the Arts Club and another to the Renaissance Society.

38. *The Octagon* 11 no. 11 (November 1939)

39. Subcommittees included Zoning & Density, Glenview Area, O'Hare Field Area, Conservation & Redevelopment, Industrial Land, Convention Center, Civic Center, Railroad Terminal, River and Lakefront, Shopping Centers and Commercial Conservation, Land Use, and Near North, with eight additional committees to be activated.

40. *Chicago Chapter AIA Bulletin* 1 no. 1 (September 1953), p. 16.

41. As that project sought additional sources of support, the long dormant Architectural Exhibition League gave its remaining funds to the microfilm project in 1953 and ceased to exist.

42. *Chicago Chapter AIA Bulletin* 2 no. 1 (September 1954), p. 9.

43. C. William Brubaker was quoted in Inland Architect 16, no. 6 (July 1970), p. 19. He summed up the dilemma: "Architects can't very well work against developers, because that way we work against ourselves. On the other hand, we have a professional responsibility to encourage a more enterprising use of property. Preservation of our past achievements is part of urban design, and this must concern both developers and architects."

44. *Inland Architect* 10, no. 1, (September 1966), p. 13

45. In the late 1970s *Inland Architect* was again becoming a financial burden. It was sold for one dollar to Harry Weese who had been providing much of the publication's financial support.

46. Elizabeth Kimball Nedved and her husband Rudolph Nedved joined the AIA in the same year. They both graduated from the Armour Institute of Technology. (From membership applications, from the AIA Archives)

Second Federal Savings
Cicero, Illinois
W. Steven Gross
Photographer: Hedrich-Blessing

Peter Elliot Studios
Chicago, Illinois
Hartshorne Plunkard, Ltd.
Photographer: Sean Kinzie

1200 Landmark Center
Omaha, Nebraska
Holabird & Root
Photographer: Tom Kessler

Hitachi Tower/Caltex House
Singapore, Singapore Strait
Murphy/Jahn, Inc.
Photographer: Tim Griffith

Kempinski Hotel
Munich, Germany
Murphy/Jahn, Inc.
Photographer: Murphy/Jahn, Inc.

Sam Yang Research Complex
Taejon, South Korea
Perkins & Will
Photographer: Youngchae Park

AT&T Corporate Headquarters/USG Building
Chicago, Illinois
Skidmore, Owings & Merrill
Photographer: Hedrich-Blessing

Exchange House
London, England
Skidmore, Owings & Merrill
Photographer: Alan Williams

Spiegel Corporate Headquarters
Downers Grove, Illinois
Skidmore, Owings & Merrill
Photographer: Hedrich-Blessing, Jon Miller

Chinatown Square
Chicago, Illinois
Harry Weese Associates
Photographer: Samuel Fein

Distinguished Building Award - *Residential*

Gray Residence
Hanover, Illinois
Brininstool + Lynch, Ltd.
Photographer: Karant + Associates, Jamie Padgett

Thompson Residence
Chicago, Illinois
Brininstool + Lynch, Ltd.
Photographer: Karant + Associates, Jamie Padgett

Highland Park Residence
Highland Park, Illinois
Stuart Cohen & Julie Hacker Architects
Photographer: Hedrich-Blessing, Jon Miller

Lake House in the Woods
Covert Township, Michigan
Davis Associates Architects & Consultants, Inc.
Photographer: Charles & Jana Davis

Cox Residence
Chicago, Illinois
Dirk Denison Architect
Photographer: Balthazar Korab

Piku Residence
Orchard Lake, Michigan
Dirk Denison Architect
Photographer: Balthazar Korab

Douglass Residence
Lake Forest, Illinois
Robert Douglass, Architects
Photographer: Robert D. Douglass

Maltz Residence
Glencoe, Illinois
Environ, Inc.
Photographer: Cable Studios, Wayne Cable

McBride Residence
Chicago, Illinois
Environ, Inc.
Photographer: Cable Studios, Wayne Cable

Urban Oasis
Chicago, Illinois
Richard Gibbons & Associates
Photographer: Richard Gibbons

Private Residence
Guilford, Connecticut
Hammond Beeby and Babka, Inc.
Photographer: Timothy Hursley, The Arkansas Office

Private Residence
Lamy, New Mexico
Hammond Beeby and Babka, Inc.
Photographer: Robert Reck Photography

Thompson Residence
Evanston, Illinois
Thomas Hickey & Associates
Photographer: Thomas Hickey, AIA

Davis Cottages
Union Pier, Michigan
Landon Architects Ltd.
Photographer: Thomas Cinoman

Devon Residence
Ada, Michigan
Lohan Associates
Photographer: Karant + Associates, Barbara Karant

Dunes House
Covert, Michigan
Nagle, Hartray & Associates, Ltd.
Photographer: Hedrich-Blessing

Meadowlake
Northfield, Illinois
Optima, Inc.
Photographer: Hedrich-Blessing

1618 North Sheridan Road
Wilmette, Illinois
Optima, Inc.
Photographer: Hedrich-Blessing

Private Residence
Chicago, Illinois
Frederick Phillips & Associates
Photographer: Bruce Van Inwegen

Siegel Residence
Chicago, Illinois
Schroeder Murchie Laya Associates, Ltd.
Photographer: Kildow Photography, William Kildow

West Washington Street Homes
South Bend, Indiana
Schroeder Murchie Laya Associates, Ltd.
Photographer: Kildow Photography, William Kildow

Galena House
Galena, Illinois
Searl and Associates, PC, Architects
Photographer: Bruce Van Inwegen

Justus Residence
Hinsdale, Illinois
Tigerman McCurry Architects
Photographer: Bruce Van Inwegen

Private Residence
La Conchita, California
Tigerman McCurry Architects
Photographer: Timothy Street Porter

Motorola Cellular Subscriber Group
Libertyville, Illinois
George T. Callas
Photographer: Steinkamp/Ballogg

Tellabs
Bolingbrook, Illinois
Heitman Architects Inc.
Photographer: Lambros Photography

Videojet
Wood Dale, Illinois
Heitman Architects Inc.
Photographer: Lambros Photography

Wheeling Township Transfer Station
Glenview, Illinois
Patrick Engineering
Photographer: William Stonecipher

Distinguished Building Award - *Institutional*

DePaul University, Parking Facility
Chicago, Illinois
Antunovich Associates Inc.
Photographer: Hedrich-Blessing, Jon Miller

Northwestern University
School of Education Building, Annenberg Hall
Evanston, Illinois
Booth/Hansen & Associates, Ltd.
Photographer: Bruce Van Inwegen

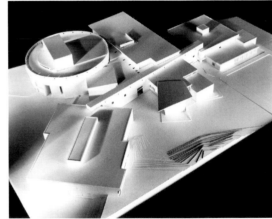

Visual & Performing Arts Center
Elgin, Illinois
Burnidge, Cassell & Associates, Inc.
Photographer: Bakstad Photographics

Heritage Center
Alma, Michigan
Cordogan, Clark & Associates Inc.
Photographer: Tim Hobbs

The Admiral, Main Entrance
Chicago, Illinois
Criezis Architects, Inc.
Photographer: Demetrios A. Criezis, AIA

Black Center for Curatorial Studies
Annandale-on-Hudson, New York
Goettsch Associates
Photographer: Esto, Peter Aaron

Taft School Athletic Facility
Watertown, Connecticut
Hammond Beeby and Babka, Inc.
Photographer: Judith Bromley

Toledo Museum of Art Renovation
Toledo, Ohio
Hammond Beeby and Babka, Inc.
Photographer: Balthazar Korab

Harold Washington Library Center
Chicago, Illinois
Hammond Beeby and Babka, Inc.
Photographer: Judith Bromley

Schoolhouse
Chicago, Illinois
Harding Associates
Photographer: Hedrich-Blessing, Jon Miller

Elmhurst City Hall
Elmhurst, Illinois
Hartshorne Plunkard, Ltd.
Photographer: Sean Kinzie

School of Architecture and Urban Planning
Milwaukee, Wisconsin
Holabird & Root
Photographer: Purcell Imaging, Ed Purcell

Alexian Brothers Medical Center, East Pavilion
Elk Grove Village, Illinois
Loebl Schlossman and Hackl, Inc.
Photographer: Steinkamp/Ballogg, James Steinkamp

Marjorie G. Weinberg Cancer Care Center
Melrose Park, Illinois
Loebl Schlossman and Hackl, Inc.
Photographer: Steinkamp/Ballogg, James Steinkamp

The Oceanarium at the John G. Shedd Aquarium
Chicago, Illinois
Lohan Associates
Photographer: Hedrich-Blessing, Nick Merrick

University of Chicago Laboratory Schools
Classroom Addition
Chicago, Illinois
Nagle, Hartray & Associates, Ltd.
Photographer: Hedrich-Blessing

Lincolnshire Village Hall
Lincolnshire, Illinois
Nagle, Hartray & Associates, Ltd.
Photographer: Hedrich-Blessing

Homewood-Flossmoor High School
Flossmoor, Illinois
O'Donnell Wicklund Pigozzi & Peterson Architects, Inc.
Photographer: Hedrich-Blessing

Lake Forest High School Additions & Renovation
Lake Forest, Illinois
O'Donnell Wicklund Pigozzi & Peterson Architects, Inc.
Photographer: David Clifton

Lincolnwood Municipal Complex
Lincolnwood, Illinois
O'Donnell Wicklund Pigozzi & Peterson Architects, Inc.
Photographer: Hedrich-Blessing

St. Raphael Catholic Church
Naperville, Illinois
O'Donnell Wicklund Pigozzi & Peterson Architects, Inc.
Photographer: Timothy Hursley, The Arkansas Office

Northern Illinois University
Hoffman Estates Education Center
Hoffman Estates, Illinois
Otis Associates, Inc. (OAI)
Photographer: PhotoSmith/Jess Smith

Barrington Area Library
Barrington, Illinois
Ross Barney + Jankowski, Inc.
Photographer: Hedrich-Blessing, Steve Hall

Cesar Chavez Elementary School
Chicago, Illinois
Ross Barney + Jankowski, Inc.
Photographer: Hedrich-Blessing, Steve Hall

SOS Children's Village
Lockport, Illinois
Rudolph & Associates, PC
Photographer: Howard N. Kaplan

Daniel F. & Ada L. Rice Children's Center
Chicago, Illinois
Skidmore, Owings & Merrill
Photographer: Hedrich-Blessing, Jon Miller

Batavia Post Office
Batavia, Illinois
Teng & Associates, Inc.
Photographer: Don DuBroff

Mt. Carmel High School Graham Center
Chicago, Illinois
Harry Weese Associates
Photographer: Samuel Fein

Vernon Area Public Library
Lincolnshire, Illinois
Yas/Fischel Partnership
Photographer: Bruce Van Inwegen

Distinguished Building Award - *Adaptive Re-Use*

DePaul University, DePaul Center
Chicago, Illinois
Daniel P. Coffey & Associates, Ltd.
Photographer: Steinkamp/Ballogg, James Steinkamp

The Rehabilitation of the Seth Peterson Cottage
Mirror Lake, Wisconsin
Eifler & Associates
Photographer: Pella, Inc.

University Hall Remodeling
Evanston, Illinois
Griskelis + Smith Architects, Ltd.
Photographer: David Clifton

Golf Cottage for the Dunes Club
New Buffalo, Michigan
Booth/Hansen & Associates, Ltd.
Photographer: Bruce Van Inwegen

Amoco Building Plaza
Chicago, Illinois
Voy Madeyski Architects Ltd.
Photographer: Wojciech Madeyski

Hyatt Regency Roissy
Roissy, France
Murphy/Jahn, Inc.
Photographer: Images Publishing, Tim Griffith

Richard D. Irwin, Inc.
Burr Ridge, Illinois
Paul B. Berger & Associates
Photographer: Jeffery Richardson

Second Federal Savings
Cicero, Illinois
W. Steven Gross
Photographer: Hedrich-Blessing

Amoco Building Entry Pavilion
Chicago, Illinois
Voy Madeyski Architects Ltd.
Photographer: Wojciech Madeyski

Exchange House
London, England
Skidmore, Owings & Merrill
Photographer: Alan Williams

10 Fleet Place
London, England
Skidmore, Owings & Merrill
Photographer: James H. Morris

Thompson Residence
Chicago, Illinois
Brininstool + Lynch, Ltd.
Photographer: Karant + Associates, Jamie Padgett

Fireplace and Wood Box for a Lake House in the Woods
Covert Township, Michigan
Davis Associates Architects & Consultants, Inc.
Photographer: Charles & Jana Davis

Adams Bath
Chicago, Illinois
Landon Architects Ltd.
Photographer: Peter Landon, AIA

1618 North Sheridan Road
Wilmette, Illinois
Optima, Inc.
Photographer: Hedrich-Blessing

Meadowlake
Northfield, Illinois
Optima, Inc.
Photographer: Hedrich-Blessing

Portico for the J. M. Brown Residence
Lake Forest, Illinois
Thomas N. Rajkovich, Architect
Photographer: Thomas N. Rajkovich

Divine Detail Award - *Residential*

Eisenberg Residence
Wilmette, Illinois
William Worn Architects
Photographer: William Worn, AIA

Divine Detail Award - *Industrial*

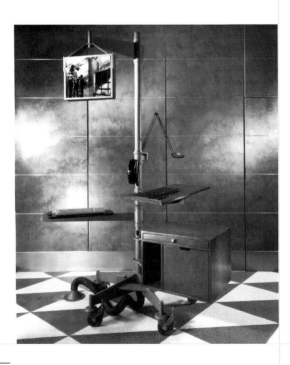

Mobile Reception Desk
Schaumburg, Illinois
Holabird & Root
Photographer: Hedrich-Blessing, Jon Miller

Schoolhouse
Chicago, Illinois
Harding Associates
Photographer: Hedrich-Blessing, Jon Miller

University of Chicago Laboratory Schools
Classroom Addition
Chicago, Illinois
Nagle, Hartray & Associates, Ltd.
Photographer: Hedrich-Blessing

Homewood-Flossmoor High School
Flossmoor, Illinois
O'Donnell Wicklund Pigozzi & Peterson Architects, Inc.
Photographer: Hedrich-Blessing

St. Patrick Mission Church
St. Charles, Illinois
Prisco Duffy & Associates, Ltd.
Photographer: Edward J. Duffy

Interior Architecture Awards - *Commercial*

Second Federal Savings
Cicero, Illinois
W. Steven Gross
Photographer: Hedrich-Blessing

Lisle Hilton Inn
Naperville, Illinois
The Gettys Group, Inc.
Photographer: Hedrich-Blessing, Jon Miller

**The Art Institute of Chicago
Servery and Dining Room**
Chicago, Illinois
Nagle, Hartray & Associates, Ltd.
Photographer: Hedrich-Blessing

American Airlines Admiral Club
Chicago, Illinois
O'Donnell Wicklund Pigozzi & Peterson Architects, Inc.
Photographer: Hedrich-Blessing, Steve Hall

Aronberg, Goldgehn, Davis & Garmisa
Chicago, Illinois
Paul B. Berger & Associates
Photographer: Hedrich-Blessing, Jon Miller

Environmental Resources Management
Deerfield, Illinois
Environ, Inc.
Photographer: Cable Studios, Wayne Cable

American Family Insurance
Madison, Wisconsin
The Environments Group
Photographer: Hedrich-Blessing, Steve Hall

Bankers Trust Company
Chicago, Illinois
The Environments Group
Photographer: Hedrich-Blessing, Steve Hall

Clausen Miller Gorman Caffrey & Witous P C
Troy, Michigan
The Environments Group
Photographer: Hedrich-Blessing, Steve Hall

RR Donnelley & Sons Company
Chicago, Illinois
Griswold Heckel & Kelly
Photographer: Hedrich-Blessing, Jon Miller

SEI Corporation
Chicago, Illinois
Griswold Heckel & Kelly
Photographer: Hedrich-Blessing, Steve Hall

Sun Microsystems
Itasca, Illinois
Interprise
Photographer: David Clifton

Henry Crown & Company
Chicago, Illinois
Larson Associates, Inc.
Photographer: Hedrich-Blessing, Nick Merrick

**Goldberg Kohn Bell Black
Rosenbloom & Moritz, Ltd.**
Chicago, Illinois
Lieber Architects
Photographer: Abby Sadin

Scariano, Kula, Ellch and Himes
Chicago, Illinois
Loebl Schlossman and Hackl, Inc.
Photographer: Hedrich-Blessing, Jon Miller

Ace Hardware Corporate Headquarters
Oak Brook, Illinois
Lohan Associates
Photographer: Hedrich-Blessing, Jon Miller

Offices of O'Donnell Wicklund Pigozzi & Peterson Architects, Inc.
Chicago, Illinois
O'Donnell Wicklund Pigozzi & Peterson Architects, Inc.
Photographer: Hedrich-Blessing, Steve Hall

M & L International
Chicago, Illinois
Pappageorge/Haymes Ltd.
Photographer: Kildow Photography, William Kildow

The Industrial Bank of Japan, Limited
Chicago, Illinois
Perkins & Will
Photographer: Hedrich-Blessing, Marco Lorenzetti

Sears Merchandise Group Home Office
Hoffman Estates, Illinois
Perkins & Will
Photographer: Steinkamp/Ballogg

TTX Company
Chicago, Illinois
Perkins & Will
Photographer: Hedrich-Blessing, Marco Lorenzetti

GATX Corporation
Chicago, Illinois
Powell/Kleinschmidt
Photographer: Hedrich-Blessing, Jon Miller

Comerica Incorporated
Detroit, Michigan
Skidmore, Owings & Merrill
Photographer: Hedrich-Blessing, Nick Merrick

Kirkland & Ellis
New York, New York
Skidmore, Owings & Merrill
Photographer: Michael Moran

Apollo Travel Service
Rolling Meadows, Illinois
VOA Associates Incorporated
Photographer: Hedrich-Blessing, Steve Hall

Ariel Capital Management, Inc.
Chicago, Illinois
VOA Associates Incorporated
Photographer: Hedrich-Blessing, Steve Hall

Brunswick Corporation
Lake Forest, Illinois
VOA Associates Incorporated
Photographer: Hedrich-Blessing, Steve Hall

Coregis Corporation
Chicago, Illinois
VOA Associates Incorporated
Photographer: Hedrich-Blessing, Steve Hall

Lester Lampert Jewelers
Chicago, Illinois
Larson Associates, Inc.
Photographer: Don DuBroff

Sugar Magnolia
Chicago, Illinois
Tigerman McCurry Architects
Photographer: Bruce Van Inwegen

**The Symphony Store for the Women's
Association of the CSO**
Chicago, Illinois
VOA Associates Incorporated
Photographer: Hedrich-Blessing, Steve Hall

The Stow Davis Studio
Chicago, Illinois
Perkins & Will
Photographer: Hedrich-Blessing, Marco Lorenzetti

Geiger International Showroom
Chicago, Illinois
VOA Associates Incorporated
Photographer: Hedrich-Blessing, Steve Hall

Room & Board
Chicago, Illinois
Office of John Vinci, Inc.
Photographer: Tony Soluri

Private Residence
Lamy, New Mexico
Hammond Beeby and Babka, Inc.
Photographer: Robert Reck

555 Residence
Glencoe, Illinois
Larson Associates, Inc.
Photographer: Hedrich-Blessing, Nick Merrick

Lofgren Residence
Green Lake, Wisconsin
Manifesto
Photographer: Hedrich-Blessing, Jon Miller

House Acquitted
Park Ridge, Illinois
pkyarchitecture
Photographer: pkyarchitecture

1728 North Wells Street
Chicago, Illinois
Weese Langley Weese Architects, Ltd.
Photographer: Karant + Associates, Jamie Padgett

Pediatric Subspecialty Clinic
Chicago, Illinois
Criezis Architects, Inc.
Photographer: Judy A. Slagle

Children's Hospital Medical Center
Cincinnati, Ohio
Eva Maddox Associates, Inc.
Photographer: Hedrich-Blessing, Jon Miller

The Art Institute of Chicago
The Ancient Galleries
Chicago, Illinois
Office of John Vinci, Inc.
Photographer: Christopher Gallagher

Vernon Area Public Library
Lincolnshire, Illinois
Yas /Fischel Partnership
Photographer: Bruce Van Inwegen

Interior Architecture Awards - *Adaptive Re-Use*

DePaul University, DePaul Center
Chicago, Illinois
Antunovich Associates Inc.
Photographer: Hedrich-Blessing, Jon Miller

**The John D. and Catherine T. MacArthur
Foundation Offices**
Chicago, Illinois
Powell/Kleinschmidt
Photographer: Hedrich-Blessing, Jon Miller

The Standard Club of Chicago
Chicago, Illinois
Powell/Kleinschmidt
Photographer: Hedrich-Blessing, Jon Miller

Continental Bank First Floor Renovation
Chicago, Illinois
Skidmore, Owings & Merrill
Photographer: Hedrich-Blessing, Nick Merrick

Burnham & Root Library Restoration
Chicago, Illinois
McClier Corporation
Photographer: Leslie Schwartz Photography

Interior Architecture Awards - *Miscellaneous*

Motorola Customer's Center for Systems Integration
Schaumburg, Illinois
Holabird & Root
Photographer: Hedrich-Blessing, Jon Miller

U2: U.S. Robotics
Skokie, Illinois
Valerio Associates, Inc.
Photographer: Karant + Associates, Barbara Karant

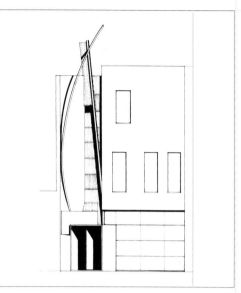

Blinderman Facade Study
Chicago, Illinois
R. C. Dahlquist & Associates

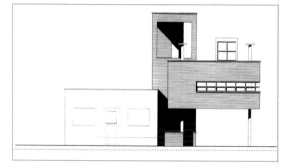

Dickson Weatherproof Nail Company
Evanston, Illinois
Frederick Phillips & Associates

Project A: Corporate Building Phases I & III
Middle East
Skidmore, Owings & Merrill
Photographer: Hedrich-Blessing

World Trade Center
Kaneohe, Hawaii
Skidmore, Owings & Merrill
Photographer: Steinkamp/Ballogg, James Steinkamp

Unbuilt Design Award - *Commercial/Residential*

Sydney Casino
Sydney, Australia
Skidmore, Owings & Merrill
Photographer: Steinkamp/Ballogg, James Steinkamp

Debord Lake House
Branson, Missouri
Rubio Durham Architects
Photographer: Rick Wood

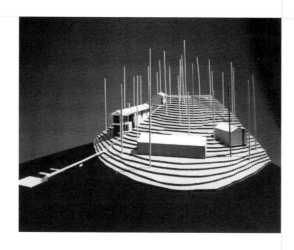

The House of Meditation
Great Mississippi River Ridge
Hanover, Illinois
Searl and Associates, PC, Architects
Photographer: Orlando Cabanban

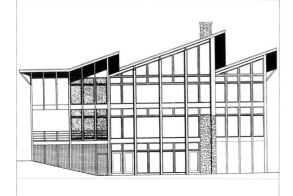

Dream House Competition
Valerio Associates, Inc.
Photographer: Orlando Cabanban

Unbuilt Design Award - *Industrial*

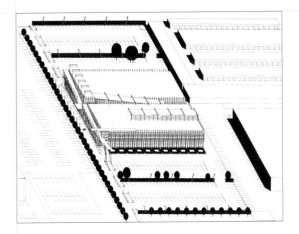

U3
Skokie, Illinois
Valerio Associates, Inc.
Photographer: Joseph M. Valerio, FAIA

Unbuilt Design Award - *Institutional*

Multi-Purpose Building
Onahan Elementary School
Chicago, Illinois
Harding Associates

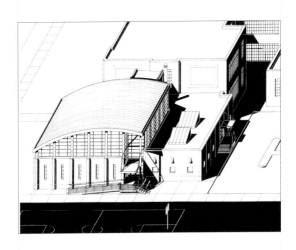

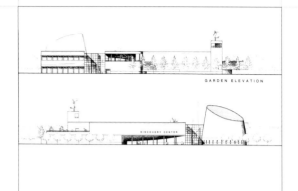

Heartland Discovery Center
Cedar, Iowa
Nagle, Hartray & Associates, Ltd.
Photographer: Orlando Cabanban

Unbuilt Design Award - *Adaptive Re-Use*

The Corner Science Store
Wellston, Missouri
Rubio Durham Architects
Photographer: Mary Jo Burke

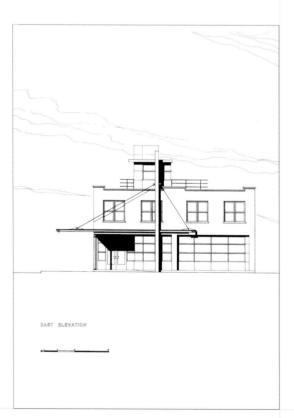

Unbuilt Design Award - *Institutional*

New Seoul Metropolitan Airport
Seoul, South Korea
Skidmore, Owings & Merrill
Photographer: Hedrich-Blessing, Robert Hart

The Towers
Southern Wisconsin
Tigerman McCurry Architects
Photographer: Bruce Van Inwegen

AIA

Distinguished Building Award

THE AMERICAN INSTITUTE OF ARCHITECTS
Chicago Chapter

Jury:

Michael Fieldman, AIA
Michael Fieldman & Partners
New York, New York

Robert J. Frasca, FAIA
Zimmer Gunsul Frasca Partnership
Portland, Oregon

Graham Gund, FAIA
Graham Gund Architects
Cambridge, Massachusetts

The Chicago Chapter AIA's Distinguished Building Award was established in 1955. The competition became a model for other AIA chapter design competitions. Nearly thirty years later, the award is intended to recognize significant achievements in the planning, design, and execution of recent building projects. Only projects by registered architects in the Chicago metropolitan area completed during the period between January 1, 1991 and May 1, 1994 were eligible.

New International Terminal
Chicago-O'Hare International Airport
Chicago, Illinois

architect:	Group One Design, Perkins & Will
design principal:	Ralph E. Johnson, AIA
project director:	James M. Stevenson, AIA
project manager:	James N. Economos, AIA
project designer:	August Battaglia, AIA
client/owner:	City of Chicago, Departments of Aviation and Public Works
general contractor:	Terminal 5 Venture, Gilbane Building Company
associates:	Heard & Associates Ltd. and Consoer Townsend & Associates
photographer:	Hedrich-Blessing

The International Terminal is intended as a 20th-century gateway to the City of Chicago, a gesture that is re-inforced by the terminal's exterior forms and sequence of interior spaces. The interior is organized on two levels to accommodate arrivals and departures. On the upper level, the ticketing lobby is the major space for departures and this space is linked to a series of increasingly smaller scaled spaces toward the departure gates. The lower level arrival spaces are organized in a similar sequence from the curbside lobby space to the skylit arrival hall.

The exterior form of the ticketing lobby is scaled to the surrounding highways and runways and serves as a marker and a gateway symbol. The strong vertical accent of the ramp control tower reinforces this symbolic gateway to passengers on arriving aircraft.

10 Fleet Place
London, England

architect: Skidmore, Owings & Merrill
Chicago, Illinois
design partner: Adrian Smith, FAIA
project partner: Alan Hinklin, AIA
senior designer: Michael Kalovitz
project manager: Neal Scotty

project team: London, England
managing partner: Thomas K. Fridstein, AIA
planning partner Roger Kallman
project manager: Tom Scheckelhoff
senior designer: Roger Kallman
designer: Dimitri Prekas
technical coordinator: Tom Janesich

client/owner: Rosehaugh Stanhope Developments PLC
general contractor: Bovis Construction Ltd.
landscape consultant: Hanna Olin
acoustics: Cerami Associates
photographer: James H. Morris

The building is located on the west side of London, close to the West End and traditional central City areas. The development is constrained beneath by the Thameslink Railway Services and Station, at grade by adjoining buildings, and above by the St. Paul's Cathedral view corridor. In addition to new shops complementing the famous pubs, a new landscaped city square provides welcome open space.

The largest building of the development at ten stories, its distinctive glass and granite facade, ground-level arcade and stepped masonry wall follow the curve of Seacoal Lane. The site consists of a raft structure spanning the British Rail lines running below the entire building. The primary public vistas are from the northeast and south entry points to Seacoal Lane. The impact of these vistas is to perceive the east wall as a compact curved surface. The other important view is from the pedestrian-only plaza to the north.

Racine Terrace

Chicago, Illinois

architect: Attila Demeter, AIA
design team: Katalin H. Demeter
client/owner: Racine Terrace Condo Association, Jeff Dahl
general contractor: AD Building Workshop
photographer: Steinkamp/Ballogg

The city's architectural tradition suggested a reinterpretation of the "urban dwelling" in the context of late 20th-century urban living and building technology.

The building is composed of three dwelling units of varied size and configuration. Two units are located on the lower levels with private landscaped yards and a shared paved courtyard. The third unit is located on the top level with two large private roof decks. The front entry stairway is the only access from the street and, with the courtyard, represents a transition from the public realm to the private realm.

The building envelope and its structural elements are composed of load-bearing, precast concrete wall panels and hollow core concrete planks. This economical construction system provides possibilities for open and light interior spaces free from columns and load-bearing walls. Exterior infill materials of glass block, bay window, and corrugated sheet metal provide texture, translucency, and plasticity to the precast concrete envelope.

Munich Order Center
Munich, Germany

architect:	Murphy/Jahn, Inc.
design team:	Helmut Jahn, FAIA; Rainer Schildknecht, AIA; and Steven Cook, AIA
client/owner:	Archimedes Gewerbe - und Buero Centrum GmbH & Co.
general contractor:	Bayerische Industrie und Gewerbe Bau GmbH & Co.
photographer:	Architekurfoto Engelhardt & Sellin

This large sporting goods showroom and exhibition center provides a variety of spaces ranging from naturally lit showrooms and offices to large exhibition spaces.

The project is on an undeveloped tract of land adjacent to large-scale railroad buildings and housing districts. The project represents a new building typology, one that requires both large expanses of exhibition space and naturally lit offices and showrooms under one roof. The solution is a series of parallel 24-meter wide building fingers springing from a technical service wall. Separating the building fingers are entrance courts, one of which extends through the building to create a park-like promenade.

The landscaped entrance courts adjoin the building foyer and provide easily identified pedestrian access to the building. Looking into the landscaped courts are support functions, such as retail shops, conference facilities, administrative offices, and a cylindrical restaurant adjacent to the promenade.

Niles West High School
Science Classroom Addition
Skokie, Illinois

architect:	O'Donnell Wicklund Pigozzi & Peterson Architects, Inc.
project principal:	Andrew D. Mendelson, AIA
director of design:	Robert D. Hunter, AIA
project manager:	Jeffery D. Foster, AIA
project designer:	Bjorn Hallsson
project architect:	Geoffrey C. Walters, AIA
client/owner:	Niles West High School
general contractor:	Pickus Construction & Equipment, Inc.
photographers:	Timothy Hursley, The Arkansas Office (exterior); Barry Rustin (interior)

The programmatic challenge was to accommodate fourteen new science classrooms plus support and preparatory spaces on a unique site. A location at the south end of the building was chosen over the east facade because it reinforced the internal flow and hierarchical logic of the existing building. It also allows the addition to break free from the existing visual context. To optimize available space, the addition responds to the angle of the site on the south and the existing rectilinear building geometry to the north, placing classrooms along the outer walls and utilizing the central "wedge" for all other required rooms. This manipulated corridor space provides areas for students to congregate. The new wing visually plays with the metaphor of science as a discipline embedded in history yet thrusting into the future.

Perry High School and Community Fitness Center

Perry, Ohio

architect:	Perkins & Will
associate architect/	
consulting engineers:	Burgess & Niple, Ltd.
design team/perkins &	
will design principal:	Ralph E. Johnson, AIA
principal-in-charge:	C. William Brubaker, FAIA
design team/	
perkins & will:	Anita Ambriz; August Battaglia, AIA; Greg Bennett; Jerry Johnson; Celeste Robbins; Steve Roberts; Bill Schmalz
design team/burgess	
& niple, ltd.	
principal in charge:	Jerry L. Keltch, AIA
client/owner:	Perry Local School District
general contractor:	Albert M. Higley Company
photographer:	Hedrich-Blessing, Nick Merrick

The project consists of a high school for 1350 students and a community fitness center, which is the first phase of a community education village. The second phase consists of an elementary and middle school, which will be connected to phase one by a bridge across a creek and natural preserve area.

The school is conceived as a series of linked elements which express the various programmatic functions. The major elements of the school, such as the library, cafeteria, theater, gymnasium, pool, and classrooms are contained in autonomous parts whose forms abstractly refer to the industrial architecture of the Lake Erie region. These elements are disposed in relation to each other and to the existing tree line to create a series of formal and informal exterior spaces.

Momochi Residential Complex
Fukuoka, Kiushu, Japan

architect: Stanley Tigerman, FAIA
design team: Roger Farris, AIA; Paul Gates; Karen Lillard, AIA; Constantine Vasilios, AIA
client/owner: Fukuoka Jisho Co., Ltd.
general contractor: Zenitaka Corp.
photographer: Esto Photo, Peter Aaron

Part of a larger, experimental housing project, the building has eighteen apartments distributed over six stories, with retail spaces located on the ground floor as specified by the program. The structure is responsive to the shifting angles of the sun, a design feature crucial to housing developments in Japan. The lobby provides the only access to a square central garden, the perimeters of which are bounded by the building. The garden remains open to the sky. The three apartments on each floor are reached by circumnavigating this central space. The garden is a metaphor for the Garden of Eden, a nostalgically sought-after original, and it is marked as such by its white grid. The exterior two-by-two meter black grid is posited as a failed attempt to suggest this original. Marked by gray ceramic tiles of different sizes, the apartments vary in their individual responses to functional concerns. The optimism intrinsic to architecture informs this design, but in the context of contemporary dislocative tendencies.

The Power House

Zion, Illinois

architect:	Stanley Tigerman, FAIA
design team:	Catherine Carr, Chris Gyder, Mark Lehmann, Tom Leung, Tom McKercher, Mark Searls, Claire Theobald
client/owner:	Commonwealth Edison
general contractor:	William A. Randolph, Inc.
consulting engineers:	Beer Gorski and Graff
photographer:	Bruce Van Inwegen

This museum is dedicated to educating the general public about the history of energy. Beginning with the quest for fire and ending with state-of-the-art robotics, this institution employs mixed media presentations to express specific intentions about varying forms of energy. The program includes designs for a permanent exhibition, temporary exhibits, and a theater.

The 400-foot-long building is in three parts. The entrance contains conventional institutional facilities, including a lobby, restrooms, a store, and a cafeteria. Here the elements of construction are designed conventionally as ducts and conduits are subordinated to the "constructive" act of building. The second part is canted and "deconstructed." Structure is exaggeratedly expressed and various forms of energy represented by ducts and conduits are kept visible. The final section of the building, where the theater and meeting rooms are located, attempts to "reconstruct" the original and fails to do so. The design of the building is inextricably linked to its use, namely the exploration of energy.

The Preserve Clubhouse
New Buffalo, Michigan

architect:	Tigerman McCurry Architects
design partner:	Margaret McCurry, FAIA
project architect:	Dante Domemella, Design Partner
client/owner:	The Preserve on the Galien, Inc.
general contractor:	K & M Contracting
photographer:	Bruce Van Inwegen

This club complex is comprised of a meeting and bath house flanked by a tennis court and swimming pool, with a small equipment building aligned along the cross axis. It was designed for use by residents of a fifty-acre, environmentally sensitive housing development surrounded by 300 acres of Galien River wetlands. The developers have pledged to the state that they will maintain this acreage in perpetuity as a wildlife preserve.

Sited among thirty housing sites overlooking the preserve, these buildings are designed in the Midwest vernacular, with clapboard siding, shingled roofs, and natural riverbed stone chimneys. The structure of the clubhouse is expressed in the exposed prefab wood trusses articulated in gray paint. White-painted wood decking and beaded board complete the coloring of the Lake Michigan resort tradition.

McEneely Residence
Evanston, Illinois

architect:	John Holbert, AIA, Holbert and Associates Architects
design team:	John Holbert, AIA; Elizabeth O'Leary; Rick O'Leary
client/owner:	Kevin and Mary McEneely
general contractor:	Grimsley Construction
photographer:	Leslie Schwartz Photography, Leslie Schwartz

The house permits lots of natural light and views from room to room, each maintaining its own spatial integrity. It is located on a narrow site, surrounded by homes with historic character from the 1920s. Because this house is larger than its neighbors, the scale was kept similar to adjacent buildings by a large roof with low eaves and a cruciform plan that screened the rear of the house from the street.

This part is a hybrid of a rural farmhouse's bi-axial cruciform plan reduced to the sideyard restrictions of a suburban townhouse lot. The plan allows light from three exposures into all of the major rooms. The front facade is kept simple, like the massing of its neighbors. The interior and exterior are related in materials and detailing to antecedents of the Arts and Crafts movement.

North Pointe
Evanston, Illinois

architect:	David C. Hovey, FAIA, Optima, Inc.
design team:	David C. Hovey, FAIA; Tom Roszak; Todd Kuhlman
client/owner:	Optima, Inc.
general contractor:	Optima, Inc.
consulting engineers:	Robert Miller, Structural; H. S. Nachman, Mechanical
photographer:	Hedrich-Blessing

North Pointe is a multi-family residential development consisting of 76 condominiums and 42 townhomes located within four separate buildings, and joined by an underground parking garage. The site gently slopes down southeastward and the two townhome buildings express this change in elevation by stepping down at every structural bay.

The odd shape of the site, due to the diagonal intersection of the three adjoining streets, suggested the trapezoidal configuration for the project. The buildings are oriented inward toward a central, two-acre landscaped courtyard featuring a lake, fountains, sundeck, and indoor/outdoor swimming pool.

Although the townhomes are of precast hollow core and the condominiums are of flat-plate, poured-in-place concrete, all of the buildings are architecturally integrated to give a visual sense of unity which enhances the sense of community.

Interior Architecture Award

THE AMERICAN INSTITUTE OF ARCHITECTS
Chicago Chapter

Jury:

Kenneth A. LeDoux, AIA
Ellerbe Becket, Inc.
Minneapolis, Minnesota

Sharon Singer
Vignelli Associates
New York, New York

Kei Yamagami
Kei Yamagami Design
San Francisco, California

In an effort to profile interior architecture as a unique profession, the Interior Architecture Award was established in 1980 to recognize outstanding excellence in the design of interior space. For award purposes, interior architecture is defined as the space within a building envelope, including the design of lighting, finishes, and furnishings. Selected from cities other than Chicago, the jurors considered a wide range of design projects completed between January 1, 1991 and May 1, 1994.

Brody Residence
Chicago, Illinois

architect:	Brininstool + Lynch, Ltd.
design team:	Bradley T. Lynch; David Brininstool, AIA; Olesegun Obasanio
client/owner:	Haim Brody
construction manager:	Brininstool + Lynch, Ltd.
carpentry consultants:	Capital Contracting
photographer:	Karant + Associates, Jamie Padgett

This project was a complete renovation of a wood-frame Victorian two-flat into a 2,400 square-foot single-family residence.

After restructuring the house and restoring the facade within the neighborhood's context, a single skylight was added to the roof. A three-story atrium was cut through the center of the house to bring a spatial relationship between the third-floor library, second-floor bedrooms, and the division of the first-floor dining and living areas. A steel and slate fireplace anchors the atrium and serves as the space's focal point.

Areas were defined through a series of elements and volumes, enhanced by seven shades of white paint, layered ceilings, and panels of translucent glass, thus directing natural light throughout the interior.

Mid-City National Bank
Chicago, Illinois

architect: Goettsch Associates
project designer: Nada Andric-Goettsch
technical director: Michael Patten, AIA
client/owner: Mid-City National Bank
general contractor: Interior Alterations
photographer: Steinkamp/Ballogg, James Steinkamp

This is a minimalist solution informed by a straightforward approach to resolving the project's requirements.

Although the bank has occupied this location for thirty years, pedestrians were unaware of the existence of this facility. The tellers were arranged along the window walls with their backs facing outside, and draperies screened the interior from the outside to provide privacy.

The solution placed tellers with work areas in the corners, thus orienting them toward the street. This corner location dictated diagonal placement of service desks and check-writing counters, while allowing dual access to the facility. Finally, the bank became a part of the streetscape, increasing its business considerably.

Hyatt Regency Roissy
Roissy, France

architect:	Murphy/Jahn, Inc.
associate architect:	Arte J. M. Charpentier
design team:	Helmut Jahn, FAIA; Gordon Beckman; Scott Pratt; Sam Scaccia, AIA
client/owner:	Hyatt International Corporation and Toa Investment Pte., Ltd.
general contractor:	Societe Auxilliare d'Entreprises de la Region Parisienne
landscape architect:	Peter Walker
photographer:	Images Publishing Group

The 400-room, four-star hotel is located in the developing area around Charles de Gaulle Airport on the periphery of Paris. The atrium lobby space creates a feeling of an "outdoor room." Large skylights and glazed endwalls define the sunlit space which flows into a garden courtyard. Linear plantings pass continuously through the glass endwall, creating a sense of unified space with the outside.

Within the atrium, architectural and landscape elements define various intimate and public spaces. The café is an elliptical "island" surrounded by water, entered by a bridge, and enclosed by a screen wall and suspended "cloud." Opaque, translucent, and transparent surfaces are juxtaposed to create interesting spatial transformations as light changes through the day.

New International Terminal
Chicago-O'Hare International Airport
Chicago, Illinois

architect:	Group One Design, Perkins & Will
design principal:	Ralph E. Johnson, AIA
managing principal:	James M. Stevenson, AIA
project manager:	James M. Economos, AIA
project designer:	August Battaglia, AIA
client/owner:	City of Chicago, Departments of Aviation and Public Works
general contractor:	Terminal 5 Venture, Gilbane Building Company
associates:	Heard & Associates Ltd. and Consoer Townsend & Associates
photographer:	Hedrich-Blessing

The International Terminal is intended as a 20th-century gateway to the City of Chicago. Both its exterior form and sequence of interior spaces reinforce this intention.

The interior is organized along two distinct linear paths to accommodate arrivals and departures. The ticketing lobby is the major space for departures on the upper level. This space is linked to a series of increasingly smaller-scaled spaces toward the departure gates. The lower level arrival spaces are organized in a similar sequence from the curbside lobby space to the skylit arrival hall.

The Rehabilitation of the Seth Peterson Cottage
Mirror Lake, Wisconsin

architect:	Eifler & Associates Architects
design principal:	John Eifler, AIA
interior architect:	Virginia Cobb
project coordinator:	Audrey Laatsch
client/owner:	The Seth Peterson Cottage Conservancy, Inc.
general contractor:	Robin Roberts Construction
photographer:	Pella, Inc.

In late 1958, Frank Lloyd Wright designed this summer cottage on Mirror Lake, Wisconsin; it was unfinished when Seth Peterson and Wright died the next year. It was purchased in 1966 by the State of Wisconsin as part of a Mirror Lake State Park expansion program. In 1985, a not-for-profit organization was formed to restore the historic but deteriorated structure for public use as an overnight retreat. A Historic Structure Report recommended that the roof, interior millwork, and mechanical, electrical, and plumbing systems be replaced and the remaining building components be incorporated with the rehabilitation plan.

The goal was to return the cottage and its interior to its condition at the time of Peterson's death and then to complete construction as originally designed by Wright. The random flagstone flooring was documented, numbered, removed, and reset so that Wright's radiant heating system could be installed. Interior improvements included the fabrication of bench seating, tables, hassocks, and kitchen cabinets according to Wright's designs.

The Grainger Ballroom
Orchestra Hall
Chicago, Illinois

architect:	Office of John Vinci, Inc.
principal:	John Vinci, FAIA
project designer:	Ward Miller
client/owner:	The Orchestral Association
general contractor:	The Orchestral Association
sound consultants:	Kirkegaard & Associates
furniture designer:	Mario Buatta, New York

Daniel Burnham's design for Orchestra Hall included a two-story, Georgian-style reception room overlooking Michigan Avenue. The ballroom's renovation returned the space to its original 1904 appearance.

For sound insulation, the arched windows were replaced with laminated glass set in mahogany frames. Mahogany and laminated glass doors between the ballroom and orchestral space were added as a barrier to sound.

A deteriorated overlay floor was replaced by oak flooring with a walnut border pattern that followed the room's plan. An extensive restoration of plaster surfaces incorporated a sound system for concerts and speaking engagements. The original stipple glazing was recreated to blend with the room's decorative features. Mirrors, chandeliers, sconces, and other furnishings were also restored.

Chicago Architecture and Design, 1923-1993: Reconfiguration of an American Metropolis
Chicago, Illinois

principal:	Tigerman McCurry Architects, Stanley Tigerman, FAIA
project architect:	Melany Telleen
associate architect:	Charles Smith
designers:	Darcy Bonner, AIA; Howard Decker, AIA; Ronald Krueck, FAIA; Kathryn Quinn; Christopher Rudolph, AIA; Dan Wheeler, AIA; Maria Whiteman, Stephen Wierzbowski
assistants:	George Drassas, Mark Lehmann, Claire Theobald
client/owner:	The Art Institute of Chicago
general contractor:	Chicago Scenic Studios, Inc.
photographer:	Bruce Van Inwegen

The exhibition installation presentation is twofold. First, each of the exhibition's eight topics are thematized in parallel gallery corridors. Second, a "time line" is superimposed in each corridor for chronological readability. Two grids disrupt each linear presentation in order to display "negative" iconic photographs about the Depression, World War I, and cultural ruptures resulting from the late 1960s. Two other grids define the beginnings and endings of each corridor to synthesize each topic photographically.

The funnel-shaped spaces compress the viewer by representing the compression understood about time itself, and the walls defining these funnel shapes are partially open in order to infer the next theme to be seen. Societally, the exhibition advances our understanding of the city by presenting the pluralism common to our age, as seen through the eyes of the anti-hero.

Thompson House
Chicago, Illinois

architect:	Brininstool + Lynch, Ltd.
design team:	Bradley T. Lynch; David Brininstool, AIA; Anthony R. Manzo
client/owner:	J. A. and Ellie Thompson
construction manager:	Brininstool + Lynch, Ltd.
photographer:	Karant + Associates, Jamie Padgett

The exterior of this single family residence is reflected in the interior through the use of concrete block wall construction. The choice of construction type is a response to the severity of the urban neighborhood, modest budget, and a desire to express manufactured materials in the most basic form, not in imitation of others. They become integral elements of the architectural volumes that define the space and function of the house.

What gives the appearance of austerity from the outside opens to a natural richness of materials and light on the interior. Birch plywood is used for both cabinets and panels. Reveals separate each change in material. The atrium skylight, in concert with the translucent panels on the south side of the house, creates an ambient light source that remains uniform day and night by incandescent backlighting. This effect will be retained even after construction on the adjacent lot.

Celtic Life Insurance
Rosemont, Illinois

architect:	The Environments Group
principal in charge:	Gina A. Berndt
project manager:	Daniel Lonergan
design manager:	Elva Rubio
project designer:	Sally Harrington
technical designer:	Rocco Tunzi
programming:	Steve Foutch
client/owner:	Celtic Group
general contractor:	Interior Development, Inc.
photographer:	Hedrich-Blessing, Steve Hall

A newly-formed division of an insurance company chose a location remote from the headquarters to foster the entrepreneurial spirit of a start-up company. This 15,000 square-foot project was designed within extremely tight budgetary constraints. An equally demanding schedule required one week for design and two weeks for construction documents. For this accomplishment, the firm was given a Special Recognition Award (see page 131).

The solution was an efficiently planned space that met the client's functional needs while introducing creative applications of low-cost materials such as plastic laminate, vinyl wallcovering, and sculpted drywall to convey the company's energetic and progressive culture. Small proportions of intense primary colors serve as visual landmarks and add a dynamic quality to the straightforward gridded plan.

Northern Trust Bank
Los Angeles, California

architect:	Krueck & Sexton Architects
design principal:	Ronald Krueck, FAIA
project principal:	Mark Sexton, AIA
project team:	John Carhart, John Ronan, and Hans Thummel
client/owner:	Northern Trust Bank
general contractor:	Environmental Contracting Corporation
consultants:	J. A. Knowles & Associates, Mechanical; Levine/Seegel Associates, Electrical; J. A. Martin & Associates, Structural; H. M. Brandston & Partners, Lighting
photographer:	Hedrich-Blessing, Marco Lorenzetti

This ground-level bank is located on a prominent street on the west side of Los Angeles and serves as a trust bank and office. The program required that the office area be separated from the banking area. The design of the grand banking hall evolved after a detailed study of the space's acoustics and limited natural light. The distinct functions of office and banking are separated by an island of conference rooms and united by a gently curving wood veneer ceiling. The convex ceiling bridges banking and office areas and reflects both natural and concealed lighting. The maple veneer ceiling and white Greek marble floor were chosen to maximize internal reflections and to express the traditional heritage of a Midwestern bank serving California.

Center for Spine, Sports, and Occupational Rehabilitation of the Rehabilitation Institute of Chicago
Chicago, Illinois

architect:	Eva L. Maddox, President, Eva Maddox Associates, Inc.
director of design:	Eileen E. Jones, Vice President
project director:	Janice Wood
project designer:	Keith Curtis
technical director:	J. D. McKibben, AIA
client/owner:	The Rehabilitation Institute of Chicago
general contractor:	LaSalle Construction Limited
photographer:	Hedrich-Blessing, Steve Hall

The design challenge began with a motion study of the human body. The resulting patterns were abstracted to form architecture and graphics throughout the space, creating an integrated solution. The overall planning process was critical to the successful joining of two adjacent buildings and the effective use of space. Color is placed unexpectedly to provide a welcoming, upbeat environmental atmosphere and inspire positive thoughts about rehabilitation. Natural light in the treatment areas was maximized and continued into the reception area through etched glass doors. Supplemental lighting complements the natural light and enhances the therapeutic environment.

Office of Perkins & Will
Chicago, Illinois

architect:	Perkins & Will
design team:	August Battaglia, AIA; Vickie DeVuono; Ralph E. Johnson, AIA; Keith Kreinik, Pauline Kurtides, Tom Mozina, Tom Peterson, Michael Poynton
client/owner:	Perkins & Will
general contractor:	Pepper Construction
photographer:	Hedrich-Blessing, Marco Lorenzetti

The central design challenge was to facilitate the restructured relationship between senior management and staff. The intrinsic character of this historic high-rise location and the timeless influence of its architect, Mies van der Rohe, formed the project's fundamental design vocabulary.

Layered planes, both horizontal and vertical, are incorporated to compose and define office and conference spaces. Juxtaposed flooring materials act as intersecting planes, weaving cross circulation patterns leading into the open studio areas. Shared horizontal work surfaces flow through glass and metal frames, physically and symbolically linking staff and management.

Wood, granite, slate, and glass were selected for their essential qualities, finished in their natural states, and then composed and detailed as separate planes sliding past one another.

Cesar Chavez Elementary School
Chicago, Illinois

architect:	Ross Barney + Jankowski, Inc.
design principal:	Carol Ross Barney, FAIA
design team:	James C. Jankowski, AIA; Wesley Hoover, AIA
client/owner:	Chicago Public Schools
general contractor:	UBM, Inc.
photographer:	Hedrich-Blessing, Steve Hall

Sited on a small and extremely narrow fragment of a city block, this public school serves Chicago's gritty, gang-infested Back-of-the-Yards neighborhood. To mitigate the unpleasant alley environment and maximize the area available for play space, the architects developed a three-story, single-loaded linear plan.

Featuring common use functions, the school's gymnasium, cafeteria, multi-purpose room, and library are housed in two-story pavilions and connected to the classroom block. Exuberant colors, textures, and forms reinforce the societal importance of the structure and convey excitement about education. A light in the pyramid's apex acts as a beacon for the community. To add warmth and hierarchy, the interior palette was expanded from concrete block and acoustical tile to include natural finished particleboard and exposed precast concrete ceilings painted sky blue. A palette of accent colors changes from bright and bold for the primary grades on the first floor to sedate and serious for the upper grades on the second and third floors.

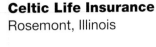

Celtic Life Insurance
Rosemont, Illinois

architect:	The Environments Group
principal in charge:	Gina A. Berndt
project manager:	Daniel Lonergan
design manager:	Elva Rubio
project designer:	Sally Harrington
technical designer:	Rocco Tunzi
programming:	Steve Foutch
client/owner:	Celtic Group
general contractor:	Interior Development, Inc.
photographer:	Hedrich-Blessing, Steve Hall

In addition to a Certificate of Merit, the jury decided to honor the project with a Special Recognition Award to distinguish the firm's outstanding ability to complete this project under extremely difficult time constraints.

To be sure, every project faces difficult schedule demands. Architects and designers everywhere work long hours to complete projects on time. But the client provided only one week for design and two weeks for construction documents. The jury believed this to be an astounding accomplishment by any office's standards. This 15,000 square-foot project was also designed within tight budgetary constraints, making this project challenging at every design stage.

AIA

Twenty-Five Year Award

THE AMERICAN INSTITUTE OF ARCHITECTS
Chicago Chapter

Jury:

George E. Danforth, FAIA
Chicago, Illinois

Carter H. Manny, Jr., FAIA
Chicago, Illinois

Pauline Saliga
Department of Architecture
The Art Institute of Chicago
Chicago, Illinois

The Twenty-Five Year Award recognizes buildings at a critical moment in their existence. This honor recognizes designs which have established not only their own identity but which also respect the rich architectural heritage of Chicago. The award was established in 1979 to recognize architectural excellence in new or adaptive re-use architectural projects completed prior to 1969. Jurors for this award evaluate historic and contemporary photographs of buildings from the recent past nominated by the Chapter, member firms, individual members, or by the Historic Resources Committee. Each nomination is evaluated on the merits of its original design, its integrity to that early intent, and the project's present use. Particular attention is paid to projects reflecting innovation and craftsmanship. Criteria for evaluating innovation include materials, siting, structural systems, floor plan, or urban planning. This year eight entries were reviewed, and two skyline landmarks of modernism in Chicago were premiated.

Lake Point Tower

Chicago, Illinois

date of design/construction:	1965-68
architect:	Schipporeit – Heinrich Associates, with Graham, Anderson, Probst & White
client/owner:	Hartnett-Shaw and Associates, Inc. and Fluor Properties
general contractor:	Crane Construction Company
photographer:	Hedrich-Blessing

Lake Point Tower is a monument to the tradition of the metal and glass skyscraper as conceived by Ludwig Mies van der Rohe in his visionary 1921 sketch of a glass tower. George Schipporeit and John C. Heinrich, two of Mies's former students and employees, designed this first skyscraper built with walls of curved glass. The young firm's first commission, Lake Point Tower has been much imitated but never equalled. Built on a small point of land that sites the 65-floor apartment tower alone on the lakefront, its bronze-toned aluminum and glass facade gleams with endless variations of light. The interaction of glass and light along the lakefront distinguishes this tower as a monument to its design and materials. Twenty-six years later when newer mirrored facades dematerialize building surfaces and the skyline, Lake Point Tower's iconic silhouette still represents a highly refined, urbane interaction between translucent glass and light. When voting to award this building, the jury lauded its reflective surface.

When completed, this glistening tower was the world's tallest apartment building. Innovative in planning, its 900 units were laid out on a cloverleaf or Y-plan determined by 120 degree angles. Spacious inside, this floorplan insures privacy, maximizes density, and provides spectacular, uninterrupted views of the lakefront horizon and the Chicago skyline. Each unit's sleeping, living, and dining areas were individually climate controlled by heating and cooling units coordinated with the wall components. The architects provided four levels of parking at the base, beneath an outdoor pool and garden.

Brunswick Building
Chicago, Illinois

date of design/construction:	1962-65
architect:	Skidmore, Owings & Merrill
partner in charge:	William Hartman, FAIA
design partner:	Bruce Graham, FAIA
senior designer:	Myron Goldsmith, FAIA
chief structural engineer:	Fazlur Khan
project manager:	Robert Henick
client/owner:	Washington-Dearborn Properties
general contractor:	George A. Fuller Company
photographers:	Orlando R. Cabanban, Paul Dunham, Hedrich-Blessing

Awarded a 1966 Citation of Merit by the Chicago Chapter AIA, the Brunswick Building represents a very early collaborative design made by three men who became synonymous with Chicago's modern skyline: Myron Goldsmith, Bruce Graham, and Fazlur Khan. At the time of its completion, the building was the largest and tallest office structure built in the Loop since the 1930s.

The reinforced concrete and glass building stands thirty-seven stories tall and occupies only fifty percent of its site, complementing the open urban space located across the street at the Daley Plaza. The Brunswick Building is significant for its structural system, the first tube structure of its type. Originally designed as a Corten Steel tube structure, the architects decided to change to a reinforced concrete tube system to preserve the Daley Plaza's material and structural identity.

AIA

Unbuilt Design Award

Jury:

Gunnar Birkerts, FAIA
Gunnar Birkerts and Associates, Inc.
Birmingham, Michigan

Karen P. Swanson, AIA
Swanson & Swanson Architects
Bloomfield Hills, Michigan

Harry Vandine, FAIA
Harley Ellington Pierce Yee
  Associates, Inc.
Southfield, Michigan

THE AMERICAN INSTITUTE OF ARCHITECTS
Chicago Chapter

The Unbuilt Design Award was established in 1991 and
resulted from the 1990 exhibition "Roads Not Taken."
None of the projects will be built, yet the award is
intended to recognize projects for the significance of
their concept and quality of design. Submitted projects
must have been commissioned by a client, however they
may include competition entries or urban design
schemes. Only registered architects from the Chicago
metropolitan area are eligible. A total of fifteen submissions were entered.

Children's Rehabilitation Center
Chicago, Illinois

architect:	Voy Madeyski Architects Ltd., Wojciech Madeyski, AIA
design team:	Wojciech Madeyski, AIA, President; Danuta Madeyski, Vice President
model builder:	Bogden Ryba
client/owner:	Gift of the Heart Foundation
photographer:	Voy Madeyski Architects Ltd.

This facility was designed for handicapped children aged 5 to 13 years, coming to Chicago from other countries to receive special treatment unavailable elsewhere. The center is designed as a combination of a hotel, school, clinic, and care center for children who may stay in the facility for periods between two weeks and six months. Children are under continuous parental supervision and medical observation. Located on a two-acre site, the building is conceived as an assemblage of colorful objects or cubes, something like giant toys, all arranged to create a mini urban environment of its own.

An intense concentration of diverse functional areas within a visually articulated environment should be conducive to the healing process. Bold colors, textures, and patterns set in a variety of interior spaces juxtaposed with exterior areas are designed to stimulate interactive play activities and to help recovery.

AIA

Divine Detail Award

THE AMERICAN INSTITUTE OF ARCHITECTS
Chicago Chapter

Jury:

Dirk S. Denison, AIA
Dirk Denison Architect
Chicago, Illinois

Gertrude Lempp Kerbis, FAIA
Chicago, Illinois

Martin Wolf, AIA
Murphy/Jahn, Inc.
Chicago, Illinois

The Divine Detail Award was established in 1988 to recognize architectural excellence in its essence. The jury looks for the ability to express a project's fundamental architectural theory or design concept in their application of a particular material, detail, or building technology. Craft must express the overall concept. New and adaptive re-use architectural projects completed between January 1, 1991 and May 1, 1994 by registered architects in the Chicago metropolitan area were eligible. Comprised of leading architects practicing in Chicago, the jury selected two winners from a total of nineteen submissions.

North Pointe
Evanston, Illinois

architect: David C. Hovey, FAIA, Optima, Inc.
design team: David C. Hovey, FAIA; Tom Roszak; Todd Kuhlman
client/owner: Optima, Inc.
general contractor: Optima, Inc.
consulting engineers: Robert Miller, Structural; H. S. Nachman, Mechanical
photographer: Hedrich-Blessing

North Pointe is a multi-family residential development consisting of 76 condominiums and 42 townhomes located within four separate buildings, and joined by an underground parking garage. The site gently slopes down southeastward and the two townhome buildings express this change in elevation by stepping down at every structural bay.

The odd shape of the site, due to the diagonal intersection of the three adjoining streets suggested the trapezoidal configuration for the project. The buildings are oriented inward toward a central, two-acre landscaped courtyard featuring a lake, fountains, sundeck, and indoor/outdoor swimming pool.

Although the townhomes are of precast hollow core and the condominiums are of flat-plate, poured-in-place concrete, all of the buildings are architecturally integrated to give a visual sense of unity which enhances the sense of community.

New International Terminal
Chicago-O'Hare International Airport
Chicago, Illinois

architect:	Group One Design, Perkins & Will
design principal:	Ralph E. Johnson, AIA
managing principal:	James M. Stevenson, AIA
project manager:	James M. Economos, AIA
project designer:	August Battaglia, AIA
client/owner:	City of Chicago, Departments of Aviation and Public Works
general contractor:	Terminal 5 Venture, Gilbane Building Company
associates:	Heard & Associates Ltd. and Consoer Townsend & Associates
photographer:	Hedrich-Blessing

The International Terminal is intended as a 20th-century gateway to the City of Chicago. Both its exterior form and sequence of interior spaces reinforce this intention.

The form, texture, and detailing of the ceiling planes was an important element in the overall design intentions of the terminal. The ceiling plane which connects the ticketing lobby to the arrival gates is a light diaphanous plane which is both engaged by and free of the structure of the building.

This ceiling plane expresses flight in its lightness and transparency and through its form heightens the sense of transition for the passenger. Its detailing allows the ceiling plane to be read as a skin applied over a structure similar to the structure of an airplane's wing. This approach to the detailing of the ceiling plane is carried throughout the terminal as a consistent theme.

AIA

Firm
Award

THE AMERICAN INSTITUTE OF ARCHITECTS
Chicago Chapter

Jury:

Gerald Cope, FAIA
Cope Linder Associates
Philadelphia, Pennsylvania

Bernard Cywinski, AIA
Bohlin Jackson Cywinski
Philadelphia, Pennsylvania

Charles E. Dagit, Jr., FAIA
Dagit-Saylor Architects
Philadelphia, Pennsylvania

The Firm Award was established in 1991 to recognize a single architectural firm for outstanding achievement in the architectural profession. Often recognized through other awards and honors, the winning firm is selected for its ongoing excellence in the design, building, technology, planning, and research, and for its notable efforts to advance the architectural profession. This year, the jury was conducted by architects from AIA Philadelphia.

Hammond Beeby and Babka was established in 1961 by James Wright Hammond, FAIA. In 1971 Mr. Hammond was joined by Thomas H. Beeby, FAIA, forming Hammond Beeby and Associates, and by Bernard Babka in 1977 when the office was incorporated under its present name.

Hammond Beeby and Babka has maintained offices in Connecticut and London as well as in Chicago. The firm is recognized for building programs into structures that are responsive to client needs and specific site conditions.

Among ongoing projects are a revitalization plan for central London's Paternoster Square, a six-building redevelopment project designed to restore a traditional street pattern, density and building scale to the historic city center. Other current projects include a 364-acre recreational and educational development for the Disney Institute in Florida, projects for Kansas State University's Farrell Library and Alumni Hall, an addition to the Oriental Institute for the University of Chicago, the renovation of Chicago's historic Fourth Presbyterian Church. Most recently, the firm was selected to design the Chicago Music and Dance Theatre, a new 1500-seat performing arts center at Cityfront Center.

Thomas H. Beeby, FAIA, is the design director for the firm. Among his projects that have received the national AIA Honor Award are the Paternoster Square Redevelopment Master Plan (1994), the Daniel F. and Ada L. Rice Building of the Art Institute of Chicago (1991), and the Conrad Sulzer Regional Library in Chicago (1987). Mr. Beeby was Dean of the Yale University School of Architecture from 1985 to 1991 and Director of the School of Architecture at the University of Illinois at Chicago from 1980 to 1985.

Bernard F. Babka, AIA, is the firm's director of technical production and office practice. He has lectured on technical aspects of architecture and served on the AIA Task Force for Quality Assurance. Trained in architecture at the Illinois Institute of Technology, he began his career with PACE Associates and worked later with Bertrand Goldberg Associates and C. F. Murphy Associates.

James Wright Hammond, FAIA (1918–1986), was founder and principal of the firm until his retirement in 1984. Trained at the Illinois Institute of Technology under Mies van der Rohe, Mr. Hammond was Eliel and Eero Saarinen's project representative for the Crow Island School while on leave from ITT. Following military service, he joined Skidmore, Owings & Merrill, becoming a partner in 1955 leaving in 1961 to form the partnership with Peter Roesch. AIA Chicago awarded several of Mr. Hammond's projects, including the Presbyterian-St. Luke's Hospital in Chicago (1966), the Northbrook (Illinois) Public Library (1970), and the First National Bank of Ripon, Wisconsin (1976).

The firm's reputation has been recently furthered internationally with the completion of the Harold Washington Library Center, the Toledo Museum of Art, the Hole-in-the-Wall Gang Camp in Connecticut, and the Paternoster Square Redevelopment Master Plan.

opposite: **Harold Washington Library**
Chicago, Illinois
Photographer: Judith Bromley

above: **Hole-in-the-Wall Gang Camp**
Westport, Connectticut
Photographer: Timothy Hursley

below: **Conrad Sulzer Library**
Chicago, Illinois
Photographer: Hedrich-Blessing

Young Architect Award

THE AMERICAN INSTITUTE OF ARCHITECTS
Chicago Chapter

Jury:

James C. Jankowski, AIA
Ross Barney + Jankowski, Inc.
Chicago, Illinois

Diane Legge Kemp, FAIA
DLK Architecture
Chicago, Illinois

Andrew Metter, AIA
A. Epstein and Sons International
Chicago, Illinois

The Young Architect Award was established in 1981 to recognize individuals between the ages of twenty-five and thirty-nine who have demonstrated through their practice and professional service general excellence and exceptional promise. Winning candidates are selected because they have been recommended as superior by established members of the architectural community. The jury determines the precise number of awards.

William D. Bradford, AIA
VOA Associates

Currently a principal and vice president and Director of Architecture for the Chicago office, William D. Bradford joined VOA Associates in 1978. His leadership and excellence in design and management has contributed significantly to the firm's growth and reputation for work in higher education, health care, corporate interiors, and municipal commissions. Mr. Bradford received his MA in architecture from the University of Illinois at Urbana-Champaign in 1978 and his BS in Architectural Studies from the same institution.

In his sixteen years of experience at VOA, Mr. Bradford has earned recognition as a principal-in-charge, design principal, project manager, and project designer for well-known landmarks of contemporary architecture. He is managing principal for the Navy Pier Reconstruction, a project won in a limited competition to rebuild this lakefront landmark with exposition space, restaurants and retail stores, a museum, indoor park, and parking space. Mr. Bradford served as senior planner and project manager for the interior design and planning of the State of Illinois Center. A multi-use facility at Clarke College in Dubuque containing facilities for a library, fine arts, offices, and a chapel won the American Institute of Steel Construction's 1987 Architectural Award of Excellence.

Mr. Bradford has participated in activities of AIA Chicago, showing his commitment to the profession and the Chapter's local goals through the Design Committee. He acted as committee coordinator for the 1986 Chapter Awards Program and rewrote the submittal requirements for all the awards. The Firm Award was created by Mr. Bradford. He was elected to the Chapter's Board of Directors in 1990, and served as vice president in 1992, when he authored the first AIA Chicago Committee Chair Handbook. Mr. Bradford is currently Chair of the Program Committee, First Vice President/President Elect of AIA Chicago, and a member of the Zoning Board of Appeals for the Village of Wilmette.

Tod Desmarais, AIA
Holabird & Root

Tod Desmarais joined Holabird & Root in 1984, and was made Associate in 1988. Prior to that, Mr. Desmarais worked at Krueck & Olsen Architects. He received his BA in Architecture from the Illinois Institute of Technology in 1981, where he remained as a Studio Instructor until he joined Holabird & Root. As a Project Designer there, he skillfully leads a collaborative team of architects and engineers in their design of very distinguished projects ranging from Holabird & Root's own offices and large-scale university buildings to corporate offices, industrial interiors, commercial showrooms, and townhouses.

Mr. Desmarais has combined his responsive sensitivity to materials, detail, proportion, color, and scale with his talented understanding of engineering to merit widespread recognition for his designs. Among many award-winning projects recognized by the AIA Chicago, his interior work for the Federal Reserve Bank of Chicago received an Interior Architecture Honor Award, his University of Illinois Digital Computer Laboratory Addition received a Distinguished Building Honor Award, and his offices for Holabird & Root received Interior Architecture and Divine Detail Awards.

In his activities to advance the profession, Mr. Desmarais has served as a jurist for the 1993 Wisconsin Society of Architects' "Young Practitioners Award" as well as for graduate and undergraduate studio reviews at the Illinois Institute of Technology.

Robert C. Robicsek, AIA
Environ, Inc.

Robert C. Robicsek, AIA was appointed vice president and principal of Environ, Inc. in 1983, two years after he joined the firm as a project manager. Mr. Robicsek's laudable architectural experience reflects the increasing diversity required by the profession. His award-winning projects range from corporate and library facilities to single and multi-family residences, interior office designs, and large government rehab projects. An honored student, Mr. Robicsek recieved his MA in Architecture from the University of Pennsylvania in 1981, and his BS in Architecture from the University of Ilinois at Urbana-Champaign in 1979.

Beyond his architectural achivement, Mr. Robicsek is widely recognized for his enthusiastic leadership, dedicated service, and pro-active involvement in civic, professional, and teaching endeavors to further the profession, the AIA, and Chicago communities. He is currently a member of the Board of Directors for the AIA Chicago, previously serving as the Chapter's delegate to the AIA Illinois. He has chaired the Government Affairs Committee, the Young Architects Committee, and the AIA Illinois Annual Awards Program, and participated in AIA Community Development Projects and joint AIA/City of Chicago Economic Development Incubator Projects. He received service awards for his volunteer work with the Chicago Architectural Assistance Center and the City of Chicago has recognized his contributions to several low-income and inner-city development projects. In addition to teaching at Triton College, Mr. Robicsek has published articles for several professional magazines, including *Architecture* and *Architectural Technology*. His work has been shown in exhibitions at the Chicago Athenaeum.

AIA

Distinguished Service Award

THE AMERICAN INSTITUTE OF ARCHITECTS
Chicago Chapter

The Distinguished Service Award is intended to recognize outstanding contributions to the architectural community by an individual or an organization. Nominations are made by Chapter members and voted on by the Board of Directors of AIA Chicago. For an organization, the award honors a singular project or an entire body of work. For an individual, the award honors a single project or the work of an entire career. This year the jury chose to honor two individuals who have very significantly shaped public and professional perceptions of historic architecture and the meaning of preservation in Chicago. Frequently they each contributed their expertise to the same restoration projects.

Anyone who has viewed exhibitions of Chicago architecture, anyone who has sought information on obscure architects, building materials, or early automobile garages, and anyone who has followed the designation of city landmarks will understand why Tim Samuelson has been chosen for this award. One can imagine this framed award resting on a bookshelf in Tim's office, appropriately surrounded by architectural fragments from lost Chicago landmarks.

Anyone who has examined the restored metalwork of Holabird and Roche's Marquette Building, Louis H. Sullivan's Stock Exchange Trading Room, or Burnham and Root's Railway Exchange Building, and anyone who has admired the entrances, storefronts, and curtain walls of the Inland Steel Building or the John Hancock Center will understand why Emil Pollack has been chosen for this award. In the words of his nominators, "His amazing career spans 60 years of exceptional service to the architectural profession and one that likely will never be equaled." AIA Chicago and the entire architectural community applaud these two individuals for their exceptional contributions to Chicago's landmark architecture.

Emil Pollack
Custom Architectural Metals, Inc.
Chicago, Illinois

Emil Pollack's working life has been devoted to metal craftsmanship, beginning with his father's trade in Hungary as a master craftsman in blacksmithing and metal fabrication. In 1920, his father joined with John Nutting to establish Illinois Bronze, where as a young boy Emil spent much of his time. In 1928, after graduating from Lane Technical School, Mr. Pollack entered architecture school at the University of Illinois where he graduated in 1933. Three years later he joined Illinois Bronze, where he worked for twenty years with Nutting. By 1960, the company had established its reputation for high-quality metalwork and craftsmanship, notable for its fabrication and installation of aluminum curtain walls. In 1968, Mr. Pollack sold his company to an employee, but only two years later he joined Sam Horowitz of the Equipment Manufacturing Company as a manager of the metal fabricating construction division. Mr. Pollack soon purchased this division and renamed it Custom Architectural Metals, Inc.

As an expert in architectural metals, Mr. Pollack has contributed enormously to the preservation of Chicago's historic architecture. He has generously given his time to instruct and demonstrate to the architectural profession the many intricacies related to the design, production, and installation of a wide range of architectural metals. When working on the 1969 Chicago City Hall restoration project, for instance, Mr. Pollack explained the art of bronze work and prepared samples of various alloys and finishes so that the restoration architects could select the precise surface most in harmony with the interior lighting. Similarly, the 1980 Marquette Building restoration project restored the bronze entrance doors and duplicated the former cast iron storefronts in aluminum.

Whether preparing decorative aluminum or bronze castings, or brass, copper, or stainless steel surfaces, Mr. Pollack has helped restore numerous storefronts, entrances and curtain walls for many of Chicago's significant buildings, including Louis H. Sullivan's Stock Exchange Trading Room at the Art Institute of Chicago and Burnham and Root's Railway Exchange Building. In addition, he has helped with metalwork for numerous post-war skyscrapers such as the Sears Tower, Inland Steel Building, the John Hancock Center, and 333 West Wacker Drive. From the testimony of his admiring supporters, many Chicago architects have benefitted from Mr. Pollack's superb craftsmanship and his profound knowledge of historic metalworking techniques and contemporary metal fabrication and installation. And beyond his expert craftsmanship, Mr. Pollack is praised among architects as a generous collaborator and teacher.

opposite: **Rookery Building**
Restoration of entrance and storefront
Chicago, Illinois

above: **Marquette Building**
Restoration of all entrances and storefronts
Chicago, Illinois

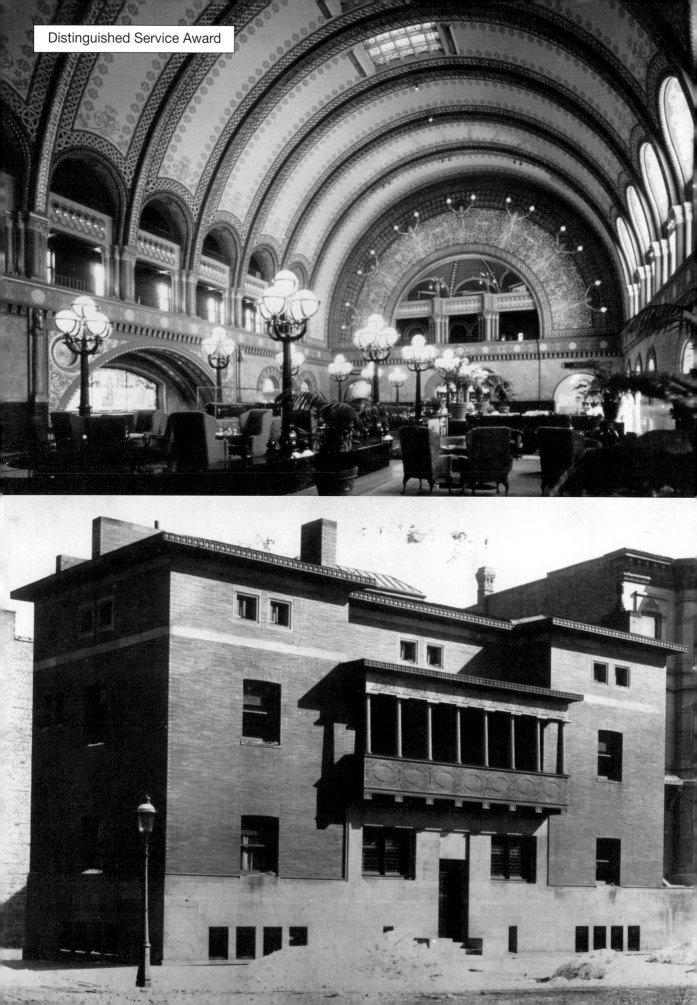

Timothy Samuelson
City of Chicago
Commission on Chicago Landmarks

For over twenty years, Timothy Samuelson has worked enthusiastically with the City of Chicago, architectural firms, and museums on matters of architecture, preservation, and historical documentation. From 1974 to 1983, Mr. Samuelson worked in the Office of John Vinci, an award-winning, restoration-oriented architectural firm. As a staff member of the Commission on Chicago Landmarks since 1983, Mr. Samuelson has documented countless buildings proposed for landmark status; provided technical and historical consultation services to property owners, architects, and contractors for the restoration of historic properties; and reviewed and evaluated building permits for alterations to historic buildings.

Samuelson has participated in the restoration and preservation of many significant historic properties. One of Mr. Samuelson's special interests is the work of Louis H. Sullivan and the firm of Adler and Sullivan. Mr. Samuelson has emphasized research and replication of period technologies and materials with an aim to adapt these specialized building crafts and materials to present-day restoration practice. Some of the many restoration projects include: John D. Van Allen & Son Department Store in Clinton, Iowa, (1912) designed by Louis H. Sullivan; Courthouse Place in Chicago, Illinois, (1892, Cook County Courthouse); the Pilgrim Baptist Church in Chicago, (1890) by Adler and Sullivan; the interior restoration of the St. Louis Union Station (1894); and the Quincy-Wells Elevated Station (1897) in Chicago. While with Vinci's office, Mr. Samuelson participated in the restoration of Burnham and Root's Monadnock Building, Sullivan's Carson Pirie Scott & Company Store, Frank Lloyd Wright's Coonley Playhouse, Adler and Sullivan's James Charnley House and Auditorium Building, and the reconstruction of their Stock Exchange Trading Room for the Art Institute of Chicago.

In addition to teaching in architectural history and preservation technology, Mr. Samuelson has published numerous articles about Chicago architecture, co-authored *Above Chicago* in 1992, and written several information booklets for the Landmarks Commission discussing houses by Bruce Goff, Walt Disney's birthplace, and the Waller Apartments, among others.

Mr. Samuelson has contributed his expertise to many museum exhibitions about Chicago architects and buildings. He curated a photo exhibition of Sullivan's work for the Van Allen Foundation in Clinton, Iowa and co-curated with Carter H. Manny, Jr. a permanent installation of architectural fragments at the Graham Foundation in Chicago. In addition, he has consulted with museums regarding the history of Chicago architecture, and he has loaned portions of his personal collection of over five-hundred architectural artifacts and documentary materials to the Art Institute of Chicago, the Chicago Architecture Foundation, Musée d'Orsay, the Chicago Historical Society, and the Cooper Hewitt Museum, among others.

opposite above: **St. Louis Union Station**
St. Louis, Missouri

opposite below: **Charnley House, ca. 1895**
Chicago, Illinois

Chicago Award

Jury:

Jocelyn Lum Frederick, AIA
Perkins & Will
Chicago, Illinois

Douglas S. Hammen, AIA
Schafer Associates
Oakbrook Terrace, Illinois

Kathleen Nagle, AIA
Holabird & Root
Chicago, Illinois

THE AMERICAN INSTITUTE OF ARCHITECTS
Chicago Chapter

The Chicago Award was established ten years ago in 1983 to recognize excellence in fourth- and fifth-year student work completed in six Midwestern architecture schools: the University of Illinois at Chicago, the University of Illinois at Urbana-Champaign, the Illinois Institute of Technology, the University of Michigan, the University of Notre Dame, and the University of Wisconsin—Milwaukee. Entries for admission are evaluated and selected at each university prior to an evaluation by the Chicago Award jury. The first place winners share a cash prize administered through the AIA Chicago Foundation. The Chicago Award was initiated by William Benn, AIA as a lasting memorial and honor to his partner, Frederick Johnck, AIA.

The jury's task of selecting the best is challenging each year because the projects vary so greatly by their project scale, program, graphic technique, presentation, and conception.

Joel T. Agacki
University of Wisconsin—Milwaukee
A Culinary Institute in the American Midwest

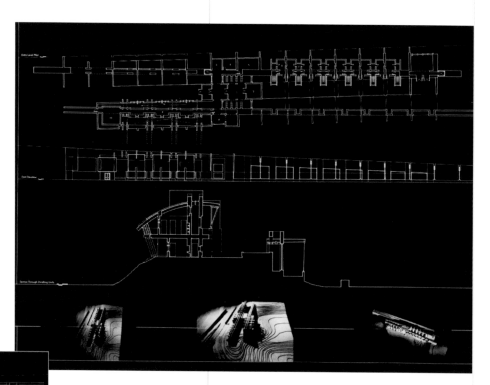

This project deals with the assault of the built form on nature. In form it is suggesting the sheer power and order required to grasp and hold space on a vast natural site with no built context. Two pure planes knife into the elevated peninsula responding to its long axis. These, along with a transparent block housing the teaching kitchen and support functions, creates the primary outdoor zones; an entry forecourt to the south and student gardens to the north, while mediating between public (restaurant) and private (students). The same peninsula that aided in giving form fights back, jarring the pieces, and in conjunction with the planes, forms secondary terraces and tertiary service herb kitchen gardens within the planes. Additive elements compose the restaurant and dwelling bars which in turn are pinned to the planes. The stick-like and frail quality of the elements contrasts sharply to the might of nature. The strict ordering of these elements locks the institute together, as well as to the peninsula.

Dillon J. Parker
University of Wisconsin—Milwaukee
Rare Books Repository

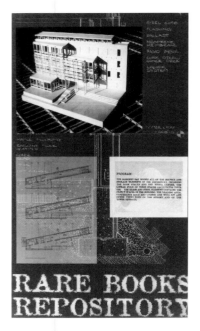

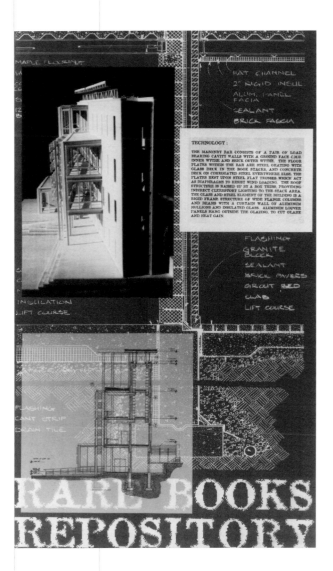

Site: The repository is located near an intersection of the city grid and the river. The masonry bar echoes the angle of a monumental tower located across the street, while a glass and steel element follows the setbacks of an adjacent municipal building. The relationship of these forms creates a plaza opposite the tower, and the reveal between the two materials provides a visual terminus for the angle of the oncoming street.

Circulation: The building is entered at the point where a walkway passes through the masonry bar. One turns and enters the glass and steel element and moves along the brick face. The stairway penetrates the wall as it ascends through the building, and the circulation connects the spaces inside and outside of the bar.

Program: The masonry bar houses all of the service and storage elements of the repository, including the book stacks and the media center. The linear form of these spaces facilitates their use. The glass and steel element contains the object spaces of the building. The reading area, conference room, and lounge offer views of the street and the nearby tower.

Technology: The masonry bar consists of a pair of load-bearing cavity walls with a ground face C.M.U. inner wythe and brick outer wythe. The floor plates within the bar are steel grating with glass deck in the book stacks and concrete deck on corrugated steel everywhere else. The plates rest upon steel flat trusses which act as diaphragms to resist wind loading. The glass and steel element of the building is a rigid frame structure of wide flange columns and beams with a curtain wall of aluminum mullions and insulated glass.

Tom Proebstle
University of Wisconsin—Milwaukee
The Fall of Icarus: Connecting the Skywalks of Minneapolis to Earth

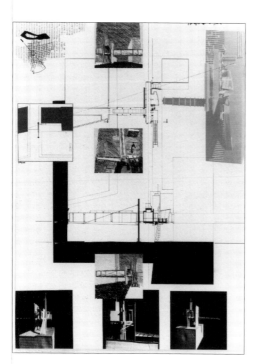 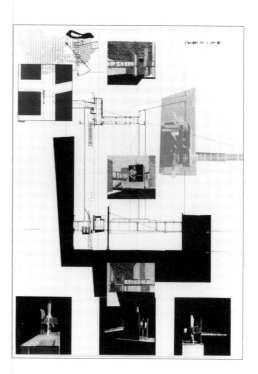

This project focused on Minneapolis's skyway and its relationship to the street and nearby buildings. Because access to the skyway is limited only to that provided by nearby buildings, the aim was to provide a physical connection from the street. Elevated nineteen feet above street level, the skyway system deprives the city's streets of activity and vitality normally associated with daily urban life. With numerous skyway connections provided throughout the central business district, commuters can enter the skyway directly from city buses or the light rail system. More importantly, pedestrians using the skyway can easily return to the street whenever they choose. Part of the solution temporarily redirects the flow of the skyway's pedestrian traffic into the axis of the street in order to emphasize the street axis over the skyway itself. As a result, the skyway depends upon the connector rather than the nearby buildings that give access to the skyway. Moreover, people walking parallel to the street along the skyway's axis are reminded of the street. While skyway pedestrians are travelling in this direction, the escalators are revealed as a convenient means to return to street level.

Patrick McGuire
University of Wisconsin—Milwaukee
Housing for People with AIDS in Chicago

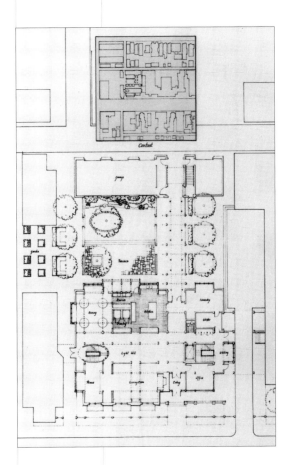

Site: The project's site is located in the center of the Lakeview neighborhood near the intersection of Belmont Avenue and Halsted Street. In 1992, 1059 cases of AIDS were reported. The project is intended for a resident group of gay men with AIDS, however the building is designed to accommodate the shifting profile of the future AIDS population.

Thesis: People with AIDS are faced with fears and anxieties above and beyond the concerns of people confronting other terminal illnesses. Their housing must address a number of specific issues:

Preserving Dignity: People with AIDS face a "cornucopia of shames." The building balances the user's relationship to the outside world with interior spaces where healing and contemplation are promoted.

Public Facade: The building's street elevation fits into the neighborhood fabric without betraying its identity. The building is neither residential nor institutional in appearance.

Privacy: The invasion of self-medical examinations, prodding, and personal inquiries threaten a sense of independence. In response, the lightwell becomes psychological cleft between the private and public spaces. Dressing areas are proposed to provide a threshold between private and semi-private spheres.

Poor Self-Image: Mirrors are located inside of medicine cabinets so that patients face a view of the garden rather than their own image of a withering self.

Fear of the Dark: AIDS patients go to sleep at night with the fear that they may not wake up. In response, the building is organized around rituals of waking and daily ablutions. Bedrooms and bathrooms provide views of the garden.

Shade Garden: Because patients taking AZT and DXT are sensitive to light, the gardens and windows of the living suite face north.

AIA

Chicago Award in Interior Architecture

THE AMERICAN INSTITUTE OF ARCHITECTS
Chicago Chapter

Jury:

John Hancock
Hancock and Hancock
Chicago, Illinois

Vicki Loevy
The McClier Corporation
Chicago, Illinois

J. D. McKibben, AIA
Eva Maddox Associates, Inc.
Chicago, Illinois

The Chicago Award in Interior Architecture was established in 1991 in an effort to support and encourage excellence in interior architecture educational programs in Midwestern colleges and universities. Offering programs in either Interior Architecture or Interior Design, this year's eight participating schools were: the University of Cincinnati, the Harrington Institute of Design, the University of Illinois at Chicago, the University of Illinois at Urbana-Champaign, Kansas State University, Lawrence Technological University, Purdue University, and the School of the Art Institute of Chicago. Awards are presented at the annual Design Excellence Awards Program.

Laurie Burns
The School of the Art Institute of Chicago
Retail Store at 60 East Walton Street

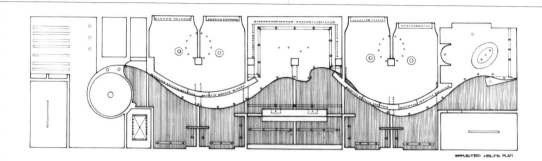

REFLECTED CEILING PLAN

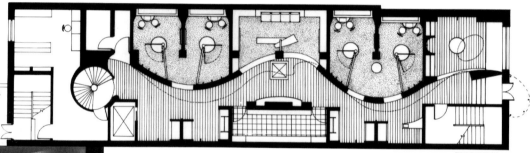

FIRST FLOOR PLAN

The idea is a new kind of retail clothing boutique using computer technology to help invent custom pieces and custom fits quickly and inexpensively. The main area of the boutique is comprised of many displays of sample garments, fabrics, shoes, and accessories. The other areas of this store contain studio areas equipped with computer terminals, desk tops, storage for fabrics, and private fitting rooms. In these studio areas the customer can sit down with a sales associate and begin the process of creating her new wardrobe with the samples and fabrics she has seen.

The building is a typical long and narrow Chicago lot. The design concept is to create a street atmosphere terminating at a grand circular staircase at the back. The length of the interior is divided into bays, bringing order to the space. The length is divided into open street display and an enclosed studio area. The space can be thought of as a large spool of thread (staircase) unravelling into space. The materials are light colored woods and metals. The finishes serve as mattes and frames for the products being displayed.

Grzegorz Lozinski
Harrington Institute of Interior Design
Paleocean Continental Seafood Restaurant

The client is a private investor who wants to open an elegant European lunch and dinner seafood restaurant to serve the surrounding cultural institutions and employees of neighboring offices. The chosen South State Street building has twenty-foot ceilings, with an emphasis on public space, traffic patterns, and ADA requirements.

Curvilinear forms are used as a metaphor for the ocean and its fauna to break up the elongated rectilinear space. The wide opening creates a mezzanine and defines walkways leading to half-circular Cafe Island. The mezzanine shape is reflected in dropped soffits illuminated by covered fluorescent strips and emphasized by a rectilinear configuration of booths and tables. Suspended stainless steel fish scales reflect and diffuse light from below, while pendant fixtures above tables spread light beams creating a twinkling effect, something like light reflected from the sea waves. A color scheme based on green-blue hues of the ocean with copper reds is used as an accent. A light oak floor and glass balustrades help to emphasize a sense of openness.

Maria DeLucia
The School of the Art Institute of Chicago
Club X

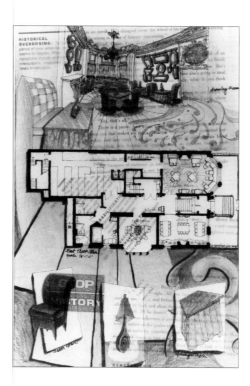

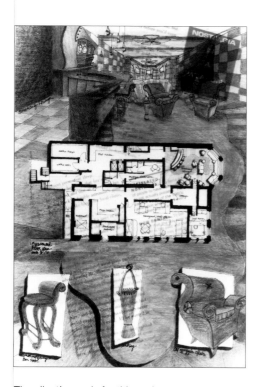

The client's needs for this project are to expand an existing upscale French restaurant to a more "hip" and affordable experience, thereby reaching a formerly excluded audience. The important changes included details sensitive to historic ornament, alterations in compliance with new ADA codes, a wheelchair-accessible entrance and bathrooms, and a club-like atmosphere to attract a young clientele.

The chief design challenge was to bring a "pop culture" concept to a building with various historic styles. In choosing to infuse the club with the viewpoint of a generation X-er, Club X reflects the generation's fragmented yet perversely nostalgic look at the past century. Here the Age of Information meets the Age of Innocence. The building is organized along a vertical time line from the first floor's Beaux-Arts influence to the third floor's funky Swing Room. The energy and variety of the rooms harkens back to Victorian sensibilities.

Toko Shiraki
The School of the Art Institute of Chicago
Three Generational Home

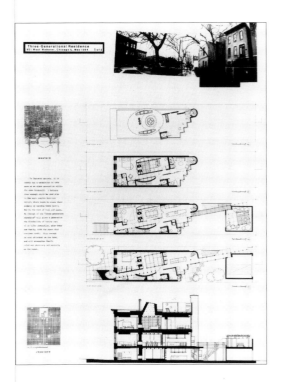

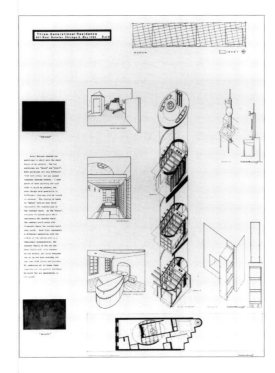

The concept is a residence which can accommodate three generations of a family. Two paintings by Matisse, *Dance* and *Music*, served as the primary impetus for the project. One represents a togetherness likened to the Western world and the other represents an openness likened to the Eastern world. Both are linked by an overall harmony. The residence seeks to establish bonds through harmony between the three generations. Remaining cost-efficient, this design strategy will strengthen physical and emotional bonds among the group.

Each floor represents a different generation within the residence, with the youngest on the top and the eldest on the bottom. They can access each other by a stairway or an elevator, meeting in the common space of the middle floor.

Acknowledgements

AIA Chicago Board of Directors 1994

John H. Nelson, AIA
President

William D. Bradford, AIA
First Vice President

Deborah Doyle, AIA
Vice President

John M. Syvertsen, AIA
Vice President

Arthur G. Salzman, AIA
Secretary

James C. Jankowski, AIA
Treasurer

Susanne Roubik, AIA
Director at Large (through December 1995)

Thomas R. Samuels, AIA
Director at Large (through December 1995)

Holly Gerberding, AIA
Director at Large (through December 1994)

Joel V. Stauber, AIA
Director at Large (through December 1994)

Alan J. Armbrust, AIA
Director

Richard E. Fencl, AIA
Director

T. Gunny Harboe, AIA
Director

Brian M. Jack, AIA
Director

Leonard Koroski, AIA
Director

Janet Hahn Lougée, AIA
Director

Thomas M. Okarma, CPCU
Director

Robert C. Robicsek, AIA
Director

Douglas B. Ross, AIA
Director

Steven S. Tousey, AIA
Director

Linda Searl, AIA
Past President

Michael F. Petersen
Professional Affiliate Director

Dirk Danker, AIA
AIA Illinois Delegate

Lou Garapolo, AIA
AIA Illinois Delegate

Gaines B. Hall, AIA
AIA Illinois Delegate

Kathleen Nagle, AIA
AIA Illinois Delegate

Leonard A. Peterson, AIA
AIA Illinois Delegate

Michael Youngman, AIA
AIA Illinois Delegate

Jon B. Masini, AIA
AIA Illinois Alternate Delegate

AIA Chicago Committee Chair and Co-Chairs 1994

Michael D. Goff, AIA
Computer

Brian M. Jack, AIA
Construction Industry Affairs

Steven S. Tousey, AIA
Corporate Architects

Alan J. Armbrust, AIA
Design

Peggy Adducci
Education

Steven L. Blonz, AIA
Helen Kessler, AIA
Environment

Robert C. Robicsek, AIA
Government Affairs

Scott C. Nelson, AIA
Terry G. Hoffman, AIA
Health

T. Gunny Harboe, AIA
Historic Resources

Janet Hahn Lougée, AIA
Interiors

Arthur G. Salzman, AIA
Membership

Thomas M. Okarma, CPCU
Office Practice

Leonard Koroski, AIA
Planning & Urban Affairs

Arthur G. Salzman, AIA
Public Relations

Richard C. DeLeo, AIA
Real Estate

Richard E. Fencl, AIA
Technical

Douglas B. Ross, AIA
Young Architects

Awards Program Committee Members 1994

Design Committee

Alan J. Armbrust, AIA
Chair

Peter Exley, AIA
Co-Chair 1994 Design Excellence Awards

Edward Keegan, AIA
Jan Kolar, AIA
Sallie Schwartzkopf, AIA
Jack Taipala, AIA
Constantine Vasilios, AIA
Daniel Watts, AIA

Representatives from Historic Resources Committee

T. Gunny Harboe, AIA
Chair

John Cinelli, AIA
Co-Chair

Kristen A. Kingsley, AIA

Timothy Barton
Awards Coordinator

Interior Architecture Committee

Janet Hahn Lougée, AIA
Chair

Kenneth P. Baker, AIA
Co-Chair

Carol LaMar, AIA
Co-Chair 1994 Design Excellence Awards

Peter Erdelyi, AIA
Angie Lee-Fasiang, AIA
Roger McFarland, AIA
J. D. McKibben, AIA
Michael Nardini, AIA
James E. Prendergast, AIA
Kevin Sherman, AIA
Patricia Sticha, AIA

Project Team

R. Stephen Sennott, Editor
Alice Sinkevitch, Executive Director
Amy L. Gold, Program Director
JNL Graphic Design, Catalogue Design
John S. Swift Co., Inc., Printing

Throughout the book, submissions and award winners are placed in alphabetical order within categories first by firm name and then by project name wherever a firm submitted more than one entry. All 1994 award winners appear in bold-face type.

The information about projects in this
publication represents the editor's and
the AIA Chicago's best efforts to identify
the architect for a given project and is
based on information provided by the firm
submitting the project for an award. Any
questions concerning further clarification
should be directed to the submitting firm.

AIA Chicago
222 Merchandise Mart Plaza
Suite 1049
Chicago, Illinois 60654

ISBN 0-929862-07-4
©1994, AIA Chicago